The Teachings of
BUDDHA

COMPILED BY
Paul Carus

St. Martin's Press   New York

A Thomas Dunne Book
An imprint of St. Martins Press

1 3 5 7 9 10 8 6 4 2

The Teachings of Buddha. This revised and abridged
edition first published in 1998.

Originally published as *The Gospel of Buddha*.

This edition abridged and revised by Diana St. Ruth.

Papers used by Rider are natural, recyclable products
made from wood grown in sustainable forests.

Printed and bound in Singapore by Tien Wah Press
PTE

A CIP catalogue record for this book
is available from the British Library

ISBN 0-312-19586-9

Contents

✳

SEATED BODHISATTVA CARVED IN RED SANDSTONE.
1ST CENTURY AD, INDIA.

PUBLISHER'S NOTE

Dr Paul Carus was among those very early Buddhists at the end of the nineteenth century who were instrumental in bringing Buddhism to the West.

He was the editor at an American publishing house which produced oriental works, and came into contact with some of the great Western translators and scholars of the day. He also met monks from Asia and the Far East who happened to be visiting America, some of whom became his dearest friends.

Carus was himself a prolific writer and scholar. His library included every available book on Buddhism in English, French and German, and one of his tales, *Karma, A Story of Buddhist Ethics*, was translated into Russian by no less a figure than Count Leo Tolstoy.

His greatest wish was to introduce Buddhism to the West in a form which was both palatable and appropriate. He deplored sectarianism in any religion and thought it unspiritual. With this in mind, he embarked upon the task of bringing together the essential strands of the Buddha's teachings common to all schools. It was a brave endeavour, and it met the approval of Soyen Shaku, a Japanese Zen master, one of those to read the text before it went to press in 1894. The book was called *The Gospel of Buddha* and turned out to be Carus's finest work.

Paul Carus went on to write and oversee many more Buddhist books and asked for the help of Soyen Shaku, but the master was too busy and sent a promising young student instead. 'My dear friend and brother,' wrote Soyen from Kamakura in 1897, 'T. Suzuki is an honest and diligent Buddhist, and I hope he will be able to assist you.' Daisetz Teitaro Suzuki proved to be a very great helper for Paul Carus and, of course, was to leave his own mark on Western Buddhism as a brilliant scholar, writer and translator.

The *Gospel* became Carus's most widely read work, and was translated into many languages. D.T. Suzuki was to translate it into Japanese, and he spoke very highly of it. The book was, indeed, a remarkable achievement and an important one, which has withstood the test of time.

This new shorter edition has been enhanced with an excellent selection of photographs, and the style of language has been brought up-to-date for the modern reader. Apart from that, Paul Carus's original work remains, as does his vision of Buddhism for the modern age in the West.

PREFACE

THE BULK OF THE CONTENTS OF THIS BOOK are derived from the old Buddhist canon. Many passages, and indeed the most important ones, are literally copied in translations from the original texts. Some are rendered rather freely in order to make them intelligible to the present generation; others have been rearranged; and still others are abbreviated. Besides the three introductory and the three concluding chapters there are only a few purely original additions, which, however, are neither mere literary embellishments nor deviations from Buddhist doctrines. Wherever the compiler has admitted modernization he has done so with due consideration and always in the spirit of a legitimate development. Additions and modifications contain nothing but ideas for which prototypes can be found somewhere among the traditions of Buddhism, and have been introduced as elucidations of its main principles.

Buddhism, like Christianity, is split up into innumerable sects, and these sects not infrequently cling to their sectarian tenets as being the main and most indispensable features of their religion. The present book follows none of the sectarian doctrines, but takes an ideal position upon which all true Buddhists may stand as upon common ground. Thus the arrangement into a harmonious and systematic form is the main original feature of this Gospel of Buddha. Considering the bulk of the various details of the Buddhist canon, however, it must be regarded as a mere compilation, and the aim of the compiler has been to treat his material in about the same way as he thinks that the author of the Fourth Gospel of the New Testament utilized the accounts of the life of Jesus of Nazareth. He has ventured to present the data of the Buddha's life in the light of their religio-philosophical importance; he has cut out most of their apocryphal adornments, especially those in which the Northern traditions abound, yet he did not deem it wise to shrink from preserving the marvellous that appears in the old records, whenever its moral seemed to justify its mention.

INTRODUCTION

I
Samsāra and Nirvāna
✸

LOOK ABOUT AND CONTEMPLATE LIFE!   1

Everything is transient and nothing endures. There is birth and death, growth and decay; there is combination and separation.   2

The glory of the world is like a flower: it stands in full bloom in the morning and fades in the heat of the day.   3

Wherever you look, there is a rushing and a struggling, and an eager pursuit of pleasure. There is a panic flight from pain and death, and hot are the flames of burning desires. The world is vanity fair, full of changes and transformations. All is Samsāra.   4

Is there nothing permanent in the world? Is there in the universal turmoil no resting place where our troubled heart can find peace? Is there nothing everlasting?   5

Oh, that we could have cessation of anxiety, that our burning desires would be extinguished! When shall the mind become tranquil and composed?   6

The Buddha, our Lord, was grieved at the ills of life. He saw the vanity of worldly happiness and sought salvation in the one thing that will not fade or perish, but will abide for ever and ever.   7

You who long for life, know that immortality is hidden in transiency. You who wish for happiness, without the sting of regret, lead a life of righteousness. You who yearn for riches, receive treasures that are eternal. Truth is wealth and a life of truth is happiness.   8

All compounds will be dissolved again, but the truths which determine all combinations and separations as laws of nature endure for ever and always. Bodies fall to dust, but the truths of the mind will not be destroyed.   9

Truth knows neither birth nor death; it has no beginning and no end. Welcome the truth. The truth is the immortal part of the mind.   10

Establish the truth in your mind, for the truth is the image of the eternal; it portrays the immutable; it reveals the everlasting; the truth gives to mortals the boon of immortality.   11

II
Truth
❁

THE THINGS OF THE WORLD and its inhabitants are subject to change. They are combinations of elements that existed before, and all living creatures are what their past actions made them; for the law of cause and effect is uniform and without exception.   1

But in the changing things there is a constancy of law, and when the law is seen there is truth. The truth lies hidden in Samsāra as the permanent in its changes.   2

Truth desires to appear; truth longs to become conscious; truth strives to know itself.   3

There is misery in the world of Samsāra; there is much misery and pain. But greater than all the misery is the bliss of truth. Truth gives peace to the yearning mind; it conquers error; it quenches the flames of desires; it leads to Nirvāna.   4

❁

PRINCE SIDDHATTHA BECOMES BUDDHA

III
The Bodhisatta's Birth
❀

THERE WAS IN KAPILAVATTHU a Sakya king, strong of purpose and reverenced by all men, a descendant of the Okkākas, who call themselves Gotama, and his name was Suddhodana or Pure-Rice. 1

His wife Māyā was beautiful as the water lily and pure in mind as the lotus. 2

The king, her husband, honored her in her holiness, and the spirit of truth, glorious and strong in his wisdom like a white elephant, descended upon her. 3

When she knew that the hour of motherhood was near, she asked the king to send her home to her parents; and Suddhodana, anxious about his wife and the child she would bear him, willingly granted her request. 4

At Lumbinī there is a beautiful grove, and when Māyā passed through it the trees were one mass of fragrant flowers and many birds were warbling in their branches. The queen, wishing to stroll through the shady walks, left her golden palanquin, and, when she reached the giant sāla tree in the midst of the grove, felt that her hour had come. She took hold of a branch. Her attendants hung a curtain about her and retired. When the pain of travail came upon her, four pure minded angels of the great Brahmā held out a golden net to receive the baby, who came forth from her right side like the rising sun bright and perfect. 5

The Brahma-angels took the child and placing him before the mother said: 'Rejoice, O queen, a mighty son has been born to you.' 6

At her couch stood an aged woman imploring the heavens to bless the
child. 7

All the worlds were flooded with light. The blind received their sight
by longing to see the coming glory of the Lord; the deaf and dumb
spoke with one another of the good omens indicating the birth of
the Buddha to be. The crooked became straight; the lame walked. All
prisoners were freed from their chains and the fires of all the hells
were extinguished. 8

No clouds gathered in the skies and the polluted streams became clear,
whilst celestial music rang through the air and the angels rejoiced
with gladness. With no selfish or partial joy but for the sake of the
law they rejoiced, for creation engulfed in the ocean of pain was now
to obtain release. 9

The cries of beasts were hushed; all malevolent beings received a loving
heart, and peace reigned on earth. Mára, the evil one, alone was
grieved and rejoiced not. 10

The Nāga kings, earnestly desiring to show their reverence for the most
excellent law, as they had paid honor to former Buddhas, now went
to greet the Bodhisatta. They scattered before him mandāra flowers,
rejoicing with heartfelt joy to pay their religious homage. 11

The royal father, pondering the meaning of these signs, was now full
of joy and now sore distressed. 12

The queen mother, beholding her child and the commotion
which his birth created, felt in her timorous heart the pangs of
doubt. 13

Now there was at that time in a grove near Lumbinī, Asita, a rishi,
leading the life of a hermit. He was a Brahman of dignified mien,
famed not only for wisdom and scholarship, but also for his skill
in the interpretation of signs. And the king invited him to see the
royal baby. 14

The seer, beholding the prince, wept and sighed deeply. And when
the king saw the tears of Asita he became alarmed and asked: 'Why
has the sight of my son caused you grief and pain?' 15

But Asita's heart rejoiced, and, knowing the king's mind to be perplexed, he addressed him, saying: 16

'The king, like the moon when full, should feel great joy, for he has acquired a wondrously noble son. 17

'I do not worship Brahmā, but I worship this child; and the gods in the temples will descend from their places of honor to adore him. 18

'Banish all anxiety and doubt. The spiritual omens manifested indicate that the child now born will bring deliverance to the whole world. 19

'Recollecting that I myself am old, on that account I could not hold my tears; for now my end is coming on and I shall not see the glory of this baby. For this son of yours will rule the world. 20

'The wheel of empire will come to him. He will either be a king of kings to govern all the lands of the earth, or will become a Buddha. He is born for the sake of everything that lives. 21

'His pure teaching will be like the shore that receives the shipwrecked. His power of meditation will be like a cool lake; and all creatures parched with the drought of lust may freely drink from it. 22

'On the fire of covetousness he will cause the cloud of his mercy to rise, so that the rain of the law may extinguish it. The heavy gates of despondency will be open, and give deliverance to all creatures ensnared in the self-entwined meshes of folly and ignorance. 23

'The king of the law has come forth to rescue from bondage all the poor, the miserable, the helpless.' 24

When the royal parents heard Asita's words they rejoiced in their hearts and named their newborn infant Siddhattha, that is 'he who has accomplished his purpose.' 25

And the queen said to her sister, Pajāpatī: 'A mother who has borne a future Buddha will never give birth to another child. I shall soon leave this world, my husband, the king, and Siddhattha, my child. When I am gone, be a mother to him.' 26

And Pajāpatī wept and promised. 27

When the queen had departed from the living, Pajāpatī took the boy Siddhattha and reared him. And as the light of the moon increases

little by little, so the royal child grew from day to day in mind and in
body; and truthfulness and love resided in his heart.   28
When a year had passed Suddhodana the king made Pajāpatī his queen
and there was never a better stepmother than she.

LIGHTING INCENSE IN THE NINH PHUC TEMPLE, VIETNAM.

IV
The Ties of Life
❋

WHEN SIDDHATTHA HAD BECOME a youth, his father desired to see him married, and he sent to all his kinsfolk, commanding them to bring their princesses that the prince might select one of them as his wife.   1

But the kinsfolk replied and said: 'The prince is young and delicate; nor has he learned any of the sciences. He would not be able to maintain our daughter, and should there be war he would be unable to cope with the enemy.'   2

The prince was not boisterous, but pensive in his nature. He loved to stay under the great jambu tree in the garden of his father, and, observing the ways of the world, gave himself up to meditation.   3

And the prince said to his father: 'Invite our kinsfolk that they may see me and put my strength to the test.' And his father did as his son requested.   4

When the kinsfolk came, and the people of the city Kapilavatthu had assembled to test the prowess and scholarship of the prince, he proved himself manly in all the exercises both of the body and of the mind, and there was no rival among the youths and men of India who could surpass him in any test, bodily or mental.   5

He replied to all the questions of the sages; but when he questioned them, even the wisest among them were silenced.   6

Then Siddhattha chose himself a wife. He selected Yasodharā, his cousin, the gentle daughter of the king of Koli. And Yasodharā was betrothed to the prince.   7

In their wedlock was born a son whom they named Rāhula which means 'fetter' or 'tie', and King Suddhodana, glad that an heir was born to his son, said: 8

'The prince having produced a son, will love him as I love the prince. This will be a strong tie to bind Siddhattha's heart to the interests of the world, and the kingdom of the Sakyas will remain under the sceptre of my descendants.'   9

With no selfish aim, but regarding his child and the people at large, Siddhattha, the prince, attended to his religious duties, bathing his body in the holy Ganges and cleansing his heart in the waters of the law. Even as men desire to give happiness to their children, so did he long to give peace to the world.   10

V
The Three Woes
❊

THE PALACE WHICH THE KING had given to the prince was resplendent with all the luxuries of India; for the king was anxious to see his son happy.   1

All sorrowful sights, all misery, and all knowledge of misery were kept away from Siddhattha, for the king desired that no troubles should come near him; he should not know that there was evil in the world.   2

But as the chained elephant longs for the wilds of the jungles, so the prince was eager to see the world, and he asked his father, the king, for permission to do so.   3

Suddhodana ordered a jewel-fronted chariot with four stately horses to be held ready, and commanded the roads to be adorned where his son would pass.   4

The houses of the city were decorated with curtains and banners, and spectators arranged themselves on either side, eagerly gazing at the heir to the throne. Thus Siddhattha rode with Channa, his charioteer, through the streets of the city, and into a country watered by rivulets and covered with pleasant trees.   5

There by the wayside they met an old man with bent frame, wrinkled face and sorrowful brow, and the prince asked the charioteer: 'Who is this? His head is white, his eyes are bleared, and his body is withered. He can barely support himself on his staff.'   6

The charioteer, much embarrassed, hardly dared speak the truth. He said: 'These are the symptoms of old age. This same man was once a suckling child, and as a youth full of sportive life; but now, as years have passed away, his beauty is gone and the strength of his life is wasted.' 7

Siddhattha was greatly affected by the words of the charioteer, and he sighed because of the pain of old age. 'What joy or pleasure can people take,' he thought to himself, 'when they know they must soon wither and pine away!' 8

And lo! while they were passing on, a sick man appeared on the wayside, gasping for breath, his body disfigured, convulsed and groaning with pain. 9

The prince asked his charioteer: 'What kind of man is this?' And the charioteer replied and said: 'This man is sick. The four elements of his body are confused and out of order. We are all subject to such conditions: the poor and the rich, the ignorant and the wise, all creatures that have bodies, are liable to the same calamity.' 10

And Siddhattha was still more moved. All pleasures appeared stale to him, and he loathed the joys of life. 11

The charioteer sped the horses on to escape the dreary sight, when suddenly they were stopped in their fiery course. 12

Four persons passed by, carrying a corpse; and the prince, shuddering at the sight of a lifeless body, asked the charioteer: 'What is this they carry? There are streamers and flower garlands; but the people that follow are overwhelmed with grief!' 13

The charioteer replied: 'This is a dead man: his body is stark; his life is gone; his thoughts are still; his family and the friends who loved him now carry the corpse to the grave.' 14

And the prince was full of awe and terror: 'Is this the only dead man,' he asked, 'or does the world contain other instances?' 15

With a heavy heart the charioteer replied: 'All over the world it is the same. He who begins life must end it. There is no escape from death.' 16

With bated breath and stammering accents the prince exclaimed: 'O worldly beings! How fatal is your delusion! Inevitably your bodies will crumble to dust, yet carelessly, unheedingly, you live on.' 17

The charioteer observing the deep impression these sad sights had made on the prince, turned his horses and drove back to the city.   18
When they passed by the palaces of the nobility, Kisā Gotamī, a young princess and niece of the king, saw Siddhattha in his manliness and

A FORM OF AVALOKITESHVARA, THE BODHISATTVA OF
COMPASSION, ADORNED WITH SEMI-PRECIOUS STONES. TIBET.

beauty, and, observing the thoughtfulness of his countenance, said:
'Happy the man that fathered you, happy the mother that nursed
you, happy the wife that calls husband this lord so glorious.'   19

The prince hearing this greeting, said: 'Happy are they that have
found deliverance. Longing for peace of mind, I shall seek the bliss
of Nirvāna.'   20

Then asked Kisā Gotamī: 'How is Nirvāna attained?' The prince paused,
and to him whose mind was estranged from wrong the answer came:
'When the fire of lust is gone out, then Nirvāna is gained; when the
fires of hatred and delusion are gone out, then Nirvāna is gained;
when the troubles of mind, arising from blind credulity, and all other
evils have ceased, then Nirvāna is gained!' Siddhattha handed her his
precious pearl necklace as a reward for the instruction she had given
him, and having returned home looked with disdain upon the
treasures of his palace.   21

His wife welcomed him and implored him to tell her the cause of his
grief. He said: 'I see everywhere the impression of change; therefore,
my heart is heavy. Beings grow old, sicken, and die. That is enough
to take away the zest of life.'   22

The king, his father, hearing that the prince had become estranged from
pleasure, was greatly overcome with sorrow and like a sword it
pierced his heart.   2

VI
The Bodhisatta's Renunciation
❀

IT WAS NIGHT. The prince found no rest on his soft pillow; he arose
and went out into the garden. 'Alas!' he cried, 'all the world is full
of darkness and ignorance; there is no one who knows how to cure
the ills of existence.' And he groaned with pain.   1

Siddhattha sat down beneath the great jambu tree and gave himself
to thought, pondering on life and death and the evils of decay.
Concentrating his mind he became free from confusion. All

low desires vanished from his heart and perfect tranquillity came
over him.   2

In this state of ecstasy he saw with his mental eye all the misery and
sorrow of the world; he saw the pains of pleasure and the inevitable
certainty of death that hovers over every being; yet men are not
awakened to the truth. And a deep compassion seized his heart.   3

While the prince was pondering on the problem of evil, he perceived
with his mind's eye under the jambu tree a lofty figure endowed with
majesty, calm and dignified. 'From where have you come, and who
may you be?' asked the prince.   4

In reply the vision said: 'I am a samana. Troubled at the thought of old
age, disease, and death I have left my home to seek the path of
salvation. All things hasten to decay; only the truth abides forever.
Everything changes, and there is no permanency; yet the words of the
Buddhas are immutable. I long for the happiness that does not
decay; the treasure that will never perish; the life that knows of no
beginning and no end. Therefore, I have destroyed all worldly
thought. I have retired into an unfrequented dell to live in solitude;
and, begging for food, I devote myself to the one thing needful.' 5

Siddhattha asked: 'Can peace be gained in this world of unrest? I am
struck with the emptiness of pleasure and have become
disgusted with lust. All oppresses me, and existence itself seems
intolerable.'   6

The samana replied: 'Where heat is, there is also a possibility of cold;
creatures subject to pain possess the faculty of pleasure; the origin of
evil indicates that good can be developed. For these things are
correlatives. Thus where there is much suffering, there will be much
bliss, if you but open your eyes to see it. Just as one who has fallen
into a heap of filth ought to seek the great pond of water covered
with lotuses which is nearby: even so you should seek for the great
deathless lake of Nirvāna to wash off the defilement of wrong. If the
lake is not sought, it is not the fault of the lake. Even so when there
is a blessed road leading one held fast by wrong to the salvation of
Nirvāna, if the road is not walked upon, it is not the fault of the road,

but of the person. And when those who are oppressed with sickness, there being a physician who can heal them, do not avail themselves of the physician's help, that is not the fault of the physician. Even so when a person oppressed by the malady of wrongdoing does not seek the spiritual guide of enlightenment, that is no fault of the evil-destroying guide.'   7

The prince listened to the noble words of his visitor and said: 'You bring good tidings, for now I know that my purpose will be accomplished. My father advises me to enjoy life and to undertake worldly duties, such as will bring honor to me and to our house. He tells me that I am too young still, that my pulse beats too full to lead a religious life.'   8

The venerable figure shook his head and replied: 'You should know that for seeking a religious life no time can be inopportune.'   9

A thrill of joy passed through Siddhattha's heart. 'Now is the time to seek religion,' he said, 'now is the time to sever all ties that would prevent me from attaining perfect enlightenment. Now is the time to wander into homelessness and, leading a mendicant's life, to find the path of deliverance.'   10

The celestial messenger heard the resolution of Siddhattha with approval.   11

'Now, indeed,' he added, 'is the time to seek religion. Go, Siddhattha, and accomplish your purpose. For you are Bodhisatta, the Buddha-elect; you are destined to enlighten the world.   12

'You are the Tathāgata, the great master, for you will fulfil all righteousness and be Dharmarāja, the king of truth. You are Bhagavat, the Blessed One, for you are called upon to become the saviour and redeemer of the world.   13

'Fulfil the perfection of truth. Though the thunderbolt descend upon your head never yield to the allurements that beguile beings from the path of truth. As the sun at all seasons pursues its own course, nor ever goes on another, even so if you forsake not the straight path of righteousness, you shall become a Buddha.   14

'Persevere in your quest and you shall find what you seek. Pursue your aim unswervingly and you shall gain the prize. Struggle earnestly and you shall conquer. The benediction of all deities, of all holy beings, of all that seek light is upon you, and heavenly wisdom guides your steps. You shall be the Buddha, our Master, and our Lord; you shall enlighten the world and save mankind from perdition.' 15

BUDDHA WITH SERPENT. 12TH CENTURY, ANGKOR WAT STYLE.

Having thus spoken, the vision vanished, and Siddhattha's heart was
filled with peace. He said to himself: 16

'I am resolved to accomplish my purpose. I will sever all the ties that
bind me to the world, and I will go out from my home to seek the
way of salvation. 17

'The Buddhas are beings whose words cannot fail: there is no departure
from truth in their speech. 18

'For as the fall of a stone thrown into the air, as the death of a
mortal, as the sunrise at dawn, as the lion's roar when he leaves his
lair, as the delivery of a woman with child, as all these things are
sure and certain – even so the word of the Buddhas is sure and
cannot fail. 19

'Truly I shall become a Buddha.' 20

The prince returned to the bedroom of his wife to take a last
farewell glance at those whom he dearly loved above all the
treasures of the earth. He longed to take the infant once more
into his arms and kiss him with a parting kiss. But the child lay in
the arms of his mother, and the prince could not lift him
without awakening both. 21

There Siddhattha stood gazing at his beautiful wife and his beloved
son, and his heart grieved. The pain of parting overcame him
powerfully. Although his mind was determined, so that nothing,
be it good or evil, could shake his resolution, the tears flowed freely
from his eyes, and it was beyond his power to check their stream. But
the prince tore himself away with a manly heart, suppressing his
feelings but not extinguishing his memory. 22

The Bodhisatta mounted his noble steed Kanthaka, and when he left
the palace, Māra stood in the gate and stopped him: 'Depart not, O
my Lord,' exclaimed Māra. 'In seven days from now the wheel of
empire will appear, and will make you sovereign over the four
continents and the two thousand adjacent islands. Therefore, stay,
my Lord.' 23

The Bodhisatta replied: 'Well do I know that the wheel of empire will
appear to me; but it is not sovereignty that I desire. I will become a

Buddha and make all the world shout for joy.'   24

Thus Siddhattha, the prince, renounced power and worldly pleasures, gave up his kingdom, severed all ties, and went into homelessness. He rode out into the silent night, accompanied only by his faithful charioteer Channa.   25

Darkness lay upon the earth, but the stars shone brightly in the heavens.   26

VII
King Bimbisāra

SIDDHATTHA HAD CUT HIS waving hair and had exchanged his royal robe for a mean dress of the color of the ground. Having sent home Channa, the charioteer, together with the noble steed Kanthaka, to king Suddhodana to bear him the message that the prince had left the world, the Bodhisatta walked along on the highroad with a beggar's bowl in his hand.   1

Yet the majesty of his mind was ill-concealed under the poverty of his appearance. His erect gait betrayed his royal birth and his eyes beamed with a fervid zeal for truth. The beauty of his youth was transfigured by holiness and surrounded his head like a halo.   2

All the people who saw this unusual sight gazed at him in wonder. Those who were in haste arrested their steps and looked back; and there was no one who did not pay him homage.   3

Having entered the city of Rājagaha, the prince went from house to house silently waiting till the people offered him food. Wherever the Blessed One came, the people gave him what they had; they bowed before him in humility and were filled with gratitude because he approached their homes.   4

Old and young people were moved and said: 'This is a noble muni! His approach is bliss. What a great joy for us!'   5

And king Bimbisāra, noticing the commotion in the city, inquired the cause of it, and when he learned the news sent one of his attendants to observe the stranger.   6

Having heard that the muni must be a Sakya and of noble family, and that he had retired to the bank of a flowing river in the woods to eat the food in his bowl, the king was moved in his heart and went to meet his mysterious guest.   7

The king found the muni of the Sakya race seated under a tree. Contemplating the composure of his face and the gentleness of his deportment, Bimbisāra greeted him reverently and said: 8

'Samana, your hands are fit to grasp the reins of an empire and should not hold a beggar's bowl. I am sorry to see you are wasting your youth. Believing that you are of royal descent, I invite you to join me in the government of my country and share my royal power. Desire for power is becoming to the noble minded, and wealth should not be despised. To grow rich and lose religion is not true gain. But one who possesses all three, power, wealth, and religion, enjoying them in discretion and with wisdom, that person I call a great master.'   9

The great Sakyamuni lifted his eyes and replied: 10

'You are known, king, to be liberal and religious, and your words are prudent. A kind man who makes good use of wealth is rightly said to possess a great treasure, but the miser who hoards up his riches will have no profit.   11

'Charity is rich in returns; charity is the greatest wealth, for though it scatters, it brings no repentance.   12

'I have severed all ties because I seek deliverance. How is it possible for me to return to the world? Those who seek religious truth, which is the highest treasure of all, must leave behind all that can concern them or draw away their attention, and must be bent upon that one goal alone. They must free their soul from covetousness and lust, and also from the desire for power.   13

'Indulge in lust but a little, and lust like a child will grow. Wield worldly power and you will be burdened with cares.   14

'Better than sovereignty over the earth, better than living in heaven, better than lordship over all the worlds, is the fruit of holiness.   15

'The Bodhisatta has recognized the illusory nature of wealth and will
not take poison as food.   16
'Will a fish that has been baited still covet the hook, or an escaped bird
love the net?   17
'Would a rabbit rescued from the serpent's mouth go back to be
devoured? Would one who has burnt his or her hand with a
torch take up the torch after dropping it to the earth? Would a blind
man who has recovered his sight desire to spoil his eyes again?   18
'The sick suffering from fever seek for a cooling medicine. Shall we
advise them to drink that which will increase the fever? Shall we

SEATED FIGURE OF THE BUDDHA, NEPAL.

quench a fire by heaping fuel upon it?   19

'Pity me not. Rather pity those who are burdened with the cares of royalty and the worry of great riches. They enjoy them in fear and trembling, for they are constantly threatened with a loss of those boons on whose possession their hearts are set, and when they die they cannot take along either their gold or the kingly diadem.   20

'My heart hankers after no vulgar profit, so I have put away my royal inheritance and prefer to be free from the burdens of life.   21

'Therefore, try not to entangle me in new relationships and duties, nor hinder me from completing the work I have begun.   22

'I regret to leave you. But I will go to the sages who can teach me truth and so find the path on which we can escape evil.   23

'May your country enjoy peace and prosperity, and may wisdom be shed upon your rule like the brightness of the noonday sun. May your royal power be strong and may righteousness be the sceptre in your hand.'   24

The king, clasping his hands with reverence, bowed down before Sakyamuni and said: 'May you obtain that which you seek, and when you have obtained it, come back and receive me as your disciple.' 25

The Bodhisatta parted from the king in friendship and goodwill, and purposed in his heart to grant his request.   26

VIII
The Bodhisatta's Search

ALĀRA AND UDDAKA were renowned as teachers among the Brahmans, and there was no one in those days who surpassed them in learning and philosophical knowledge.   1

The Bodhisatta went to them and sat at their feet. He listened to their doctrines of the ūtman or self, which is the ego of the mind and the doer of all doings. He learned their views of the transmigration of souls and of the law of karma; how the souls of bad people had to suffer by being reborn in people of low caste, in animals, or in hell, while those who purified themselves by libations, by sacrifices, and by self-mortification would become kings, or Brahmans, or devas, so as to rise higher and higher in the grades of existence. He studied their incantations and offerings and the methods by which they attained deliverance of the ego from material existence in states of ecstasy. 2

Alāra said: 'What is that self which perceives the actions of the five roots of mind, touch, smell, taste, sight, and hearing? What is that which is active in the two ways of motion, in the hands and in the feet? The problem of the soul appears in the expressions "I say," "I know and perceive," "I come," and "I go" or "I will stay here." Your soul is not your body; it is not your eye, not your ear, not your nose, not your tongue, nor is it your mind. The I is the one who feels the touch in your body. The I is the smeller in the nose, the taster in the tongue, the seer in the eye, the hearer in the ear, and the thinker in the mind. The I moves your hands and your feet. The I is your soul. Doubt in the existence of the soul is irreligious, and without discerning this truth there is no way of salvation. Deep speculation will easily involve the mind; it leads to confusion and unbelief; but a purification of the soul leads to the way of escape. True deliverance is reached by removing from the crowd and leading a hermit's life, depending entirely on alms for food. Putting away all desire and clearly recognizing the nonexistence of matter, we reach a state of perfect emptiness. Here we find the condition of immaterial life. As the muñja grass when freed from its horny case, as a sword when drawn from its scabbard, or as the wild bird escaped from its prison, so the ego, liberating itself from all limitations, finds perfect release. This is true deliverance, but those only who will have deep faith will learn.' 3

The Bodhisatta found no satisfaction in these teachings. He replied: 'People are in bondage because they have not yet removed the idea of the ego. 4

'The thing and its quality are different in our thought, but not in reality. Heat is different from fire in our thought, but you cannot remove heat from fire in reality. You say that you can remove the qualities and leave the thing, but if you think your theory to the end, you will find that this is not so.   5

'Are not beings organisms of many aggregates? Are we not composed of various attributes? We consist of the material form, of sensation, of thought, of dispositions, and, lastly, of understanding. That which people call the ego when they say "*I am*" is not an entity behind the attributes; it originates by their co-operation. There is mind; there is sensation and thought, and there is truth; and truth is mind when it walks in the path of righteousness. But there is no separate ego-soul outside or behind the thought of beings. Those who believe that the ego is a distinct being have no correct conception of things. The very search for the ātman is wrong; it is a wrong start and it will lead you in a false direction.   6

'How much confusion of thought comes from our interest in self, and from our vanity when thinking "*I am so great,*" or "*I have done this wonderful deed?*" The thought of your ego stands between your rational nature and truth; banish it, and then you will see things as they are. Those who think correctly will rid themselves of ignorance and acquire wisdom. The ideas "*I am*" and "*I shall be*" or "*I shall not be*" do not occur to a clear thinker.   7

'Moreover, if our ego remains, how can we attain true deliverance? If the ego is to be reborn in any of the three worlds, be it in hell, upon earth, or be it even in heaven, we shall meet again and again the same inevitable doom of sorrow. We shall remain chained to the wheel of individuality and shall be implicated in egotism and wrong.   8

'All combination is subject to separation, and we cannot escape birth, disease, old age, and death. Is this a final escape?'   9

Uddaka said: 'Consider the unity of things. Things are not their parts, yet they exist. The members and organs of your body are not your ego, but your ego possesses all these parts. What, for instance, is the Ganges? Is the sand the Ganges? Is the water the Ganges? Is the near bank the Ganges? Is the farther bank the Ganges? The Ganges is a mighty river and it possesses all these several qualities. Exactly so is our ego'.   10

But the Bodhisatta replied: 'Not so, sir! If we except the water, the sand, the near bank and the farther bank, where can we find any Ganges? In the same way I observe the activities of human beings in their harmonious union, but there is no ground for an ego outside its parts'.   11

The Brahman sage, however, insisted on the existence of the ego, saying: 'The ego is the doer of our deeds. How can there be karma

THE BUDDHA CARVED OUT OF ROCK AT YUNKANG, SHANSI PROVINCE, CHINA. 5TH CENTURY.

without a self as its performer? Do we not see around us the effects of karma? What makes people different in character, station, possessions, and fate? It is their karma, and karma includes merit and demerit. The transmigration of the soul is subject to its karma. We inherit from former existences the evil effects of our evil deeds and the good effects of our good deeds. If that were not so, how could we be different?'   12

The Tathāgata meditated deeply on the problems of transmigration and karma, and found the truth that lies in them.   13

'The doctrine of karma,' he said, 'is undeniable, but your theory of the ego has no foundation.   14

'Like everything else in nature, the life of man is subject to the law of cause and effect. The present reaps what the past has sown, and the future is the product of the present. But there is no evidence of the existence of an immutable ego-being, of a self which remains the same and migrates from body to body. There is rebirth but no transmigration.   15

'Is not this individuality of mine a combination, material as well as mental? Is it not made up of qualities that sprang into being by a gradual evolution? The five roots of sense-perception in this organism have come from ancestors who performed these functions. The ideas which I think, came to me partly from others who thought them, and partly they rise from combinations of the ideas in my own mind. Those who have used the same sense-organs, and have thought the same ideas before I was composed into this individuality of mine are my pervious existences; they are my ancestors as much as the *I* of yesterday is the father of the *I* of today, and the karma of my past deeds conditions the fate of my present existence.   16

'Supposing there were an ātman that performs the actions of the senses, then if the door of sight were torn down and the eye plucked out, that ātman would be able to peep through the larger aperture and see the forms of its surroundings better and more clearly than before. It would be able to hear sounds better if the ears were torn away; smell better if the nose were cut off; taste better if the tongue were pulled out; and feel better if the body were destroyed.   17

'I observe the preservation and transmission of character; I perceive the truth of karma, but see no ātman whom your doctrine makes the doer of your deeds. There is rebirth without the transmigration of a self. For this ātman, this self, this ego in the "I say" and in the "I will" is an illusion. If this self were a reality, how could there be an escape from selfhood? The terror of hell would be infinite, and no release could be granted. The evils of existence would not be due to our ignorance and wrongdoing, but would constitute the very nature of our being.'   18

And the Bodhisatta went to the priests officiating in the temples. But the gentle mind of the Sakyamuni was offended at the unnecessary cruelty performed on the altars of the gods. He said: 19

'Ignorance only can make these men prepare festivals and hold vast meetings for sacrifices. Far better to revere the truth than try to appease the gods by shedding blood.   20

'What love can a man possess who believes that the destruction of life will atone for evil deeds? Can a new wrong expiate old wrongs! And can the slaughter of an innocent victim blot out the evil deeds of mankind? This is practising religion by the neglect of moral conduct.   21

'Purify your hearts and cease to kill; that is true religion.   22

'Rituals have no efficacy; prayers are vain repetitions; and incantations have no saving power. But to abandon covetousness and lust, to become free from evil passions, and to give up all hatred and ill will, that is the right sacrifice and the true worship.'   23

IX
Uruvelā, the Place of Mortification
❋

THE BODHISATTA WENT IN SEARCH of a better system and came to a settlement of five bhikkhus in the jungle of Uruvelā; and when the Blessed One saw the life of those five men, virtuously keeping in check their senses, subduing their passions, and practising austere self-discipline, he admired their earnestness and joined their company. 1

With holy zeal and a strong heart, the Sakyamuni gave himself up to meditative thought and rigorous mortification of the body. Whereas the five bhikkhus were severe, the Sakyamuni was severer still, and they revered him, their junior, as their master.   2

So the Bodhisatta continued for six years patiently torturing himself and suppressing the wants of nature. He trained his body and exercised his mind in the modes of the most rigorous ascetic life. At last, he ate each day one hemp-grain only, seeking to cross the ocean of birth and death and to arrive at the shore of deliverance.   3

And when the Bodhisatta was oppressed with hunger, Māra, the Evil One, approached him and said: 'You are emaciated from fasts, and death is near. What good is your exertion? Deign to live, and you will be able to do good works.' But the Sakyamuni made reply: 'Let the flesh waste away, if but the mind becomes more tranquil and attention more steadfast. What is life in this world? Death in battle is better to me than that I should live defeated.'   4

And Māra withdrew, saying: 'For seven years I have followed the Blessed One step by step, but I have found no fault in the Tathāgata'.   5

The Bodhisatta was thin and weak and his body was like a withered branch; but the frame of his holiness spread in the surrounding countries, and people came from great distances to see him and receive his blessing.   6

However, the Holy One was not satisfied. Seeking true wisdom he did not find it, and he came to the conclusion that mortification would not extinguish desire nor afford enlightenment in ecstatic contemplation.   7

Seated beneath a jambu tree, he considered the state of his mind and the fruits of his mortification. His body had become weaker, but his fasts had not advanced him in his search for salvation, and therefore when he saw that it was not the right path, he proposed to abandon it.   8

He went to bathe in the Neranjara river, but when he strove to leave the water he could not rise on account of his weakness. Then noticing the branch of a tree and taking hold of it, he raised himself and left the stream. But while returning to his abode, he staggered and fell to

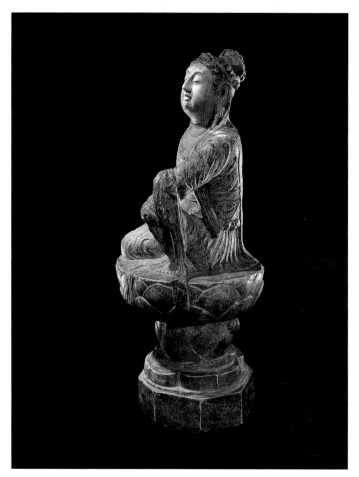

THE BODDHISATTVA GUANYIN, WHO LATER BECAME
KNOWN AS THE GODDESS OF MERCY.
TANG DYNASTY, CHINA, AD 618-906.

the ground, and the five bhikkhus thought he was dead. 9

There was a chief herdsman living near the grove whose eldest daughter was called Nandā; and Nandā happened to pass by the spot where the Blessed One had swooned, and bowing down before him she offered him rice-milk and he accepted the gift. When he had partaken of the rice-milk all his limbs were refreshed, his mind became clear again, and he was strong to receive the highest enlightenment. 10

After this occurrence, the Bodhisatta again took some food. His disciples, having witnessed the scene of Nandā and observing the change in his mode of living, were filled with suspicion. They were convinced that Siddhattha's religious zeal was flagging and that he whom they had till now revered as their Master had become oblivious of his high purpose. 11

When the Bodhisatta saw the bhikkhus turning away from him, he felt sorry for their lack of confidence, and was aware of the loneliness in which he lived. 12

Suppressing his grief he wandered on alone, and his disciples said, 'Siddhattha leaves us to seek a more pleasant abode.' 13

X
Māra the Evil One
❋

THE HOLY ONE DIRECTED HIS STEPS to that blessed Bodhi tree beneath whose shade he was to accomplish his search. 1

As he walked, the earth shook and a brilliant light transfigured the world. 2

When he sat down the heavens resounded with joy and all living beings were filled with good cheer. 3

Māra alone, lord of the five desires, bringer of death and enemy of truth, was grieved and rejoiced not. With his three daughters, Tanhā, Ragā and Arati, the tempters, and with his host of evil demons, he went to the place where the great samana sat. But

Sakyamuni heeded him not.   4

Māra uttered fear-inspiring threats and raised a whirlwind so
that the skies were darkened and the ocean roared and trembled. But
the Blessed One under the Bodhi tree remained calm and feared not.
The Enlightened One knew that no harm could befall him.   5

The three daughters of Māra tempted the Bodhisatta, but he paid
no attention to them, and when Māra saw that he could kindle
no desire in the heart of the victorious samana, he ordered all the
evil spirits at his command to attack him and overawe the great
muni.   6

But the Blessed One watched them as one would watch the harmless
games of children. All the fierce hatred of the evil spirits was of no
avail. The flames of hell became wholesome breezes of perfume, and
the angry thunderbolts were changed into lotus blossoms.   7

When Māra saw this, he fled away with his army from the Bodhi tree,
whilst from above a rain of heavenly flowers fell, and voices of good
spirits were heard: 8

'Behold the great muni! his heart unmoved by hatred. The wicked
Māra's host against him did not prevail. Pure is he and wise, loving
and full of mercy.   9

'As the rays of the sun drown the darkness of the world, so those who
persevere in their search will find the truth and the truth will
enlighten them.'   10

XI
Enlightenment
❀

THE BODHISATTA, having put Māra to flight, gave himself up to
meditation. All the miseries of the world, the evils produced by evil
deeds and the suffering arising therefrom, passed before his mental
eye, and he thought: 1

'Surely if living creatures saw the results of all their evil deeds, they
would turn away from them in disgust. But selfhood blinds them,

and they cling to their obnoxious desires.   2

'They crave pleasure for themselves and they cause pain to others; when death destroys their individuality, they find no peace; their thirst for existence abides and their selfhood reappears in new births.   3

'Thus they continue to move in the coil and can find no escape from the hell of their own making. And how empty are their pleasures, how vain are their endeavours! Hollow like the plantain tree and without contents like the bubble.   4

'The world is full of sorrow, because it is full of lust. Men go astray because they think that delusion is better than truth. Rather than truth they follow error, which is pleasant to look at in the beginning but in the end causes anxiety, tribulation, and misery.'   5

And the Bodhisatta began to expound the Dharma. The Dharma is the truth. The Dharma is the sacred law. The Dharma is religion. The Dharma alone can deliver us from error, from wrong and from sorrow.   6

Pondering on the origin of birth and death, the Enlightened One recognized that ignorance was the root of all evil; and these are the links in the development of life, called the twelve nidānas: 7

From ignorance proceeds impulses; from impulses proceeds consciousness; from consciousness proceeds name and form; from name and form proceeds the six sense fields, that is, the five senses and the mind; from the six sense fields proceeds contact; from contact proceeds sensation; from sensation proceeds craving; from craving proceeds clinging; from clinging proceeds the becoming process; from becoming proceeds birth; from birth proceeds old age and death.   8

The cause of all sorrow lies at the very beginning; it is hidden in ignorance. Remove ignorance and you will destroy the wrong desires that rise from ignorance; destroy these desires and you will wipe out the wrong perception that rises from them. Destroy wrong perception and there is an end of errors in individualized beings. Destroy the errors in individualized beings and the illusions of the six sense fields will disappear. Destroy illusions and the contact with

THE BODHISATTVA AVALOKITESHVARA. ONE INTERPRETATION
OF HIS NAME IS THE 'LORD WHO LOOKS DOWN'.
9-10TH CENTURY, INDOCHINA.

things will cease to give rise to misconception. Destroy misconception and you do away with thirst. Destroy thirst and you will be free of all morbid clinging. Remove clinging and you destroy the selfishness of selfhood. If the selfishness of selfhood is destroyed you will be above birth, old age, disease, and death, and you will escape all suffering. 9

The Enlightened One saw the four noble truths which point out the path that leads to Nirvāna or the extinction of self: 10

The first noble truth is the existence of sorrow. 11
The second noble truth is the cause of suffering. 12
The third noble truth is the cessation of sorrow. 13
The fourth noble truth is the eightfold path that leads to the cessation of sorrow. 14

This is the Dharma. This is the truth. And the Enlightened One uttered this stanza: 15

'Though many births I sought in vain
The Builder of this House of Pain.
Now, Builder, thee I plainly see!
This is the last abode for me.
Thy gable's yoke and rafters broke,
My heart has peace. All lust will cease.' 16

There is self and there is truth. Where self is, truth is not. Where truth is, self is not. Self is the fleeting error of samsāra; it is individual separateness and that egotism which engenders envy and hatred. Self is the yearning for pleasure and the lust after vanity. Truth is the correct comprehension of things; it is the permanent and everlasting, the real in all existence, the bliss of righteousness. 17

The existence of self is an illusion, and there is no wrong in this world, no vice, no evil, except what flows from the assertion of self. 18

The attainment of truth is possible only when self is recognized as an illusion. Righteousness can be practised only when we have freed our mind from passions of egotism. Perfect peace can dwell only where all vanity has disappeared.   19

XII
Brahmā's Request
❀

THE BLESSED ONE, having attained Buddhahood while resting under the shepherd's Nigrodha tree on the banks of the river Nerañjarā, pronounced this solemn utterance: 1

'How blest in happy solitude
Are they who hear of truth the call!
How blest to be both kind and good,
To practice self-restraint to all!
How blest from passion to be free,
All sensuous joys to let pass by!
Yet highest bliss enjoyeth they
Who quit the pride of "I am I."   2

'I have recognized the deepest truth, which is sublime and peace-giving, but difficult to understand; for most people move in a sphere of worldly interests and find their delight in worldly desires.   3

'Worldlings will not understand the doctrine, for to them there is happiness in selfhood only, and the bliss that lies in a complete surrender to truth is unintelligible to them.   4

'They will call resignation what to the enlightened mind is the purest joy. They will see annihilation where the perfected one finds immortality. They will regard as death what the conqueror of self knows to be life everlasting.   5

'The truth remains hidden from those who are in the bondage of hate and desire. Nirvāna remains incomprehensible and mysterious to the vulgar whose minds are beclouded with worldly interests. Should I preach the doctrine and mankind not comprehend it, it would bring me only fatigue and trouble.'   6

Māra, the Evil One, on hearing the words of the Blessed Buddha, approached and said: 'You have attained the highest bliss and it is time for you to enter into the final Nirvāna.'   7

Then Brahmā Sahampati descended from the heavens and having worshipped the Blessed On, said: 8

'Alas! the world must perish, should the Holy One, the Tathāgata, decide not to teach the Dharma.   9

'Be merciful to those that struggle; have compassion upon the sufferers; pity the creatures who are hopelessly entangled in the snares of sorrow.   10

'There are some beings that are almost free from the dust of worldliness. If they hear not the doctrine preached, they will be lost. But if they hear it, they will believe and be saved.'   11

The Blessed One, full of compassion, looked with the eye of a Buddha upon all sentient creatures, and he saw among them beings whose minds were but scarcely covered by the dust of worldliness, who were of good disposition and easy to instruct. He saw some who were conscious of the dangers of lust and wrongdoing.   12

And the Blessed One said to Brahmā Sahampati: 'Wide open is the door of immortality to all who have ears to hear. May they receive the Dharma with faith.'   13

And the Blessed One turned to Māra, saying: 'I shall not pass into the final Nirvāna, Evil One, until there are not only brothers and sisters of an Order, but also lay disciples of both sexes, who shall have become true hearers, wise, well trained, ready and learned, versed in the scriptures, fulfilling all the greater and lesser duties, correct in life, walking according to the precepts – until they, having themselves learned the doctrine, shall be able to give information to others concerning it, make it known, establish it, open it, minutely explain it, and make it clear – until they, when others start vain doctrines, shall be able to vanquish and refute them, and so to spread the wonder-working truth abroad. I shall not die until the pure religion of truth shall have become successful, prosperous, widespread, and popular in all its full extent – until, in a word, it shall have been well proclaimed!'   14

Then Brahmā Sahampati understood that the Blessed One had granted his request and would preach the doctrine.   15

✿

THANGKA PAINTING. THE IMAGE IS PAINTED ON LINEN, USING
VEGETABLE- AND MINERAL-BASED PIGMENTS. TIBET.

THE FOUNDATION OF THE KINGDOM OF RIGHTEOUSNESS

XIII
Upaka

❀

Now the Blessed One thought: 'To whom shall I preach the doctrine first? My old teachers are dead. They would have received the good news with joy. But my five disciples are still alive. I shall go to them, and to them shall I first proclaim the gospel of deliverance.' 1

At that time the five bhikkhus were staying in the Deer Park at Benares, and the Blessed One rose and journeyed to their abode, not thinking of their unkindness in having left him at a time when he was most in need of their sympathy and help, but mindful only of the services which they had ministered to him, and pitying them for the austerities which they practised in vain. 2

Upaka, a young Brahman and a Jain, a former acquaintance of Siddhattha, saw the Blessed One on his way to Benares and, amazed at the majesty and sublime joyfulness of his appearance, said: 'Your countenance, friend, is serene; your eyes are bright and indicate purity and blessedness.' 3

The holy Buddha replied: 'I have obtained deliverance by the extinction of self. My body is chastened, my mind is free from desire, and the deepest truth has taken abode in my heart. I have obtained Nirvāna, and this is the reason that my countenance is serene and my eyes are bright. I now desire to found the kingdom of truth upon earth, to give light to those who are enshrouded in darkness and to open the gate of deathlessness.' 4

Upaka replied: 'You profess then, friend, to be Jina, the conqueror of the world, the absolute one and the holy one.' 5

The Blessed One said: 'Jinas are all those who have conquered self and the passions of self, those alone are victors who control their minds and abstain from evil. Therefore, Upaka, I am the Jina.' 6

Upaka shook his head. 'Venerable Gotama,' he said, 'your way lies over there,' and taking another road, he went away. 7

XIV
The Sermon at Benares

ON SEEING THEIR OLD TEACHER approach, the five bhikkhus agreed among themselves not to greet him, nor to address him as a master, but by his name only. 'For,' so they said, 'he has broken his vow and has abandoned holiness. He is no bhikkhu but Gotama, and Gotama has become a man who lives in abundance and indulges in the pleasures of worldliness.' 1

But when the Blessed One approached in a dignified manner, they involuntarily rose from their seats and greeted him in spite of their resolution. Still they called him by his name and addressed him as 'friend Gotama.' 2

The Blessed One said: 'Do not call the Tathāgata by his name nor address him as "friend," for his is the Buddha, the Holy One. The Buddha looks with a kind heart equally on all living beings, and they therefore call him "Father." To disrespect a father is wrong; to despise him is shameful. 3

'The Tathāgata,' the Buddha continued, 'does not seek salvation in austerities, but neither does he for that reason indulge in worldly pleasures, nor live in abundance. The Tathāgata has found the middle path. 4

'There are two extremes, bhikkhus, which the man who has given up the world ought not to follow – the habitual practice, on the one hand, of self-indulgence which is unworthy, vain and fit only for the worldly-minded – and the habitual practice, on the other hand, of self-mortification, which is painful, useless and unprofitable. 5

'Neither abstinence from fish or flesh, nor going naked, nor shaving the head, nor wearing matted hair, nor dressing in a rough garment,

nor covering oneself with dirt, nor sacrificing to Agni, will cleanse
anyone who is not free from delusions   6

'Reading the Vedas, making offerings to priests, or sacrifices to the
gods, self-mortification by heat or cold, and many such penances
performed for the sake of immortality, these do not cleanse those
who are not free from delusions.   7

'A middle path, bhikkhus, avoiding the two extremes, has been
discovered by the Tathāgata – a path which opens the eyes and
bestows understanding, which leads to peace of mind, to the higher
wisdom, to full enlightenment, to Nirvāna!   8

'Let me teach you, bhikkhus, the middle path. By suffering, the
emaciated devotee produces confusion and sickly thoughts.
Mortification is not conducive even to worldly knowledge; how
much less to a triumph over the senses!   9

'Those who fill their lamps with water will not dispel the darkness,
and those who try to light a fire with rotten wood will fail. And how
can anyone be free from self by leading a wretched life, if that
person does not succeed in quenching the fires of lust, if that
person still hankers after either worldly or heavenly pleasures. But
those in whom self has become extinct are free from lust; they
will desire neither worldly nor heavenly pleasures, and the
satisfaction of their natural wants will not defile them. However, let
them be moderate, let them eat and drink according to the needs of
the body.   10

'Sensuality is enervating; the self-indulgent are slaves to their passions,
and pleasure-seeking is degrading and vulgar.   11

'But to satisfy the necessities of life is not evil. To keep the body in
good health is a duty, for otherwise we shall not be able to trim the
lamp of wisdom, and keep our mind strong and clear. Water
surrounds the lotus flower, but does not wet its petals.   12

'This is the middle path, bhikkhus, that keeps aloof from both
extremes.'   13

And the Blessed One spoke kindly to his disciples, pitying them for
their errors, and pointing out the uselessness of their endeavors,

and the ice of ill will that chilled their hearts melted away under the gentle warmth of the Master's persuasion.   14

Now the Blessed One set the wheel of the most excellent law rolling,

GANDHARA GREY SCHIST HEAD OF THE BUDDHA,
C. 3-4TH CENTURY BC.

and he began to preach to the five bhikkhus, opening to them the gate of immortality, and showing them the bliss of Nirvāna.   15

The Buddha said: 16

'The spokes of the wheel are the rules of pure conduct: justice is the uniformity of their length; wisdom is the tire; modesty and thoughtfulness are the hub in which the immovable axle of truth is fixed.   17

'Those who recognize the existence of suffering, its cause, its remedy, and its cessation have fathomed the four noble truths. They will walk in the right path.   18

'Right views will be the torch to light their way. Right aspirations will be their guide. Right speech will be their dwelling place on the road. Their gait will be straight, for it is right behavior. Their refreshments will be the right way of earning their livelihood. Right efforts will be their steps: right thoughts their breath; and right contemplation will give them the peace that follows in their footprints.   19

'Now, this, bhikkhus, is the noble truth concerning suffering: 20

'Birth is attended with pain – decay is painful, disease is painful, death is painful. Union with the unpleasant is painful, painful is separation from the pleasant, and any craving that is unsatisfied, that too is painful. In brief, bodily conditions which spring from attachment are painful.   21

'Now this, bhikkhus, is the noble truth concerning the origin of suffering: 22

'It is that craving which causes the renewal of existence, accompanied by sensual delight, seeking satisfaction now here, now there, the craving for the gratification of the passions, the craving for a future life, and the craving for happiness in this life.   23

'Now this, bhikkhus, is the noble truth concerning the destruction of suffering: 24

'It is the destruction, in which no passion remains, of this very thirst; it is the laying aside of, the being free from, the dwelling no longer upon this thirst.   25

'Now this, bhikkhus, is the noble truth concerning the way which

leads to the destruction of sorrow. It is this noble eightfold path, that is to say: 26
'Right views, right aspirations, right speech, right behavior, right livelihood, right effort, right thoughts, and right contemplation. 27
'This, then, bhikkhus, is the noble truth concerning the destruction of sorrow. 28
'By the practice of loving kindness I have attained liberation of heart, and thus I am assured that I shall never return in renewed births. I have even now attained Nirvāna.' 29
And when the Blessed One had thus set the royal chariot-wheel of truth rolling onward, a rapture thrilled through all the universes. 30
The devas left their heavenly abodes to listen to the sweetness of the truth; the holy beings that had parted from life crowded around the great teacher to receive the glad tidings; even the animals of the earth felt the bliss that rested upon the words of the Tathāgata: and all the creatures of the host of sentient beings, gods, men, and beasts, hearing the message of deliverance, received and understood it in their own language. 31
And when the doctrine was propounded, the venerable Kondañña, the oldest one among the five bhikkhus, discerned the truth with his mental eye, and he said: 'Truly, you have found the truth!' Then the other bhikkhus too, joined him and exclaimed: 'Truly, you are the Buddha, you have found the truth.' 32
And the devas and holy beings and all the good spirits of the departed generations that had listened to the sermon of the Tathāgata, joyfully received the doctrine and shouted: 'Truly, the Blessed One has founded the kingdom of righteousness. The Blessed One has moved the earth; he has set the wheel of Truth rolling, which no one in the universe, god or human being, can ever turn back. The kingdom of Truth will be preached upon earth; it will spread; and righteousness, goodwill, and peace will reign among mankind.' 33

XV
Kassapa
❀

AT THAT TIME THERE LIVED in Uruvelā the Jatilas, Brahman hermits with matted hair, worshipping the fire and keeping a fire dragon; and Kassapa was their chief.   1

Kassapa was renowned throughout all India, and his name was honored as one of the wisest men on earth and an authority on religion.   2

And the Blessed One went to Kassapa of Uruvelā, the Jatila, and said: 'Let me stay a night in the room where you keep your sacred fire.'   3

Kassapa, seeing the Blessed One in his majesty and beauty, thought to himself: 'This is a great muni and a noble teacher. Should he stay overnight in the room where the sacred fire is kept, the serpent will bite him and he will die.' And he said: 'I do not object to your staying overnight in the room where the sacred fire is kept, but the serpent lives there; he will kill you and I should be sorry to see you perish.'   4

But the Buddha insisted and Kassapa admitted him to the room.   5

And the Blessed One sat down with his body erect, surrounding himself with watchfulness.   6

In the night the dragon came to the Buddha, belching forth in rage his fiery poison, and filling the air with burning vapor, but could do him no harm, and the fire consumed itself while the World-honored One remained composed. And the venomous fiend became enraged so that he died in his anger.   7

When Kassapa saw the light shining from the room he said: 'Alas, what misery! Truly, the countenance of Gotama the great Sakyamuni is beautiful, but the serpent will destroy him.'   8

In the morning the Blessed One showed the dead body of the fiend to Kassapa, saying: 'His fire has been conquered by my fire.'   9

And Kassapa thought to himself. 'Sakyamuni is a great samana and possesses high powers, but he is not holy like me.'   10

There was in those days a festival, and Kassapa thought: 'The people

will come here from all parts of the country and will see the great
Sakyamuni. When he speaks to them, they will believe in him and
abandon me.' And he grew envious.   11
When the day of the festival arrived, the Blessed One retired and did
not come to Kassapa. And Kassapa went to the Buddha on the next
morning and said: 'Why did the great Sakyamuni not come?'   12
The Tathāgata replied: 'Did you not think, Kassapa, that it would be
better if I stayed away from the festival?'   13
And Kassapa was astonished and thought: 'Great is Sakyamuni; he can

DETAIL OF A SCROLL PAINTING (*THANGKA*). IMAGES ON
THANGKAS CAN SERVE AS VISUAL REMINDERS OF BUDDHIST
TEACHINGS. MONGOLIA.

read my most secret thoughts, but he is not holy like me.'   14

And the Blessed One said. 'You see the truth, but do not accept it because of the envy that dwells in your heart. Is envy holiness? Envy is the last remnant of self that has remained in your mind. You are not holy, Kassapa; you have not yet entered the path.'   15

And Kassapa gave up his resistance. His envy disappeared, and bowing down before the Blessed One, he said: 'Lord, let me receive the ordination from the Blessed One.'   16

And the Blessed One said: 'You Kassapa, are chief of the Jatilas. Go, then, first and inform them of your intention, and let them do as they think fit.'   17

Then Kassapa went to the Jatilas and said: 'I am anxious to lead a religious life under the direction of the great Sakyamuni, who is the Enlightened One, the Buddha. Do as you think best.'   18

And the Jatilas replied: 'We have conceived a profound affection for the great Sakyamuni, and if you will join his brotherhood, we will do likewise.'   19

The Jatilas of Uruvelā now flung their paraphernalia of fire worship into the river and went to the Blessed One.   20

Nadī Kassapa and Gayā Kassapa, brothers of the great Uruvelā Kassapa, powerful men and chieftains among the people, were dwelling below on the stream, and when they saw the instruments used in fire worship floating in the river, they said: 'Something has happened to our brother.' And they came with their folk to Uruvelā. Hearing what had happened, they, too, went to the Buddha.   21

The Blessed One, seeing that the Jatilas of Nadī and Gayā, who had practised severe austerities and worshipped fire, had now come to him, preached a sermon on fire, and said: 22

'Everything, Jatilas, is burning. The eye is burning, all the senses are burning, thoughts are burning. They are burning with the fire of lust. There is anger, there is ignorance, there is hatred, and as long as the fire finds inflammable things upon which it can feed, so long will it burn, and there will be birth and death, decay, grief, lamentation, suffering, despair, and sorrow. Considering this, disciples of the Dharma will see the four noble truths and walk in the eightfold path of holiness. They will become wary of their eye, wary of all their senses, wary of their thoughts. They will divest themselves of passion and become free. They will be delivered from selfishness and attain the blessed state of Nirvāna.'   23

And the Jatilas rejoiced and took refuge in the Buddha, the Dharma, and the Sangha.   24

XVI
The Sermon at Rājagaha

AND THE BLESSED ONE having stayed some time in Uruvelā went to Rājagaha, accompanied by a great number of bhikkhus, many of whom had been Jatilas before, and the great Kassapa, chief of the Jatilas and formerly a fire worshipper, went with him.   1

When the Magadha king, Seniya Bimbisāra, heard of the arrival of Gotama Sakyamuni, of whom the people said, 'He is the Holy One, the blessed Buddha, guiding people as a driver curbs bullocks, the teacher of high and low,' he went out surrounded with his counsellors and generals and came to the grove where the Blessed One was.   2

There they saw the Blessed One in the company of Kassapa, the great religious teacher of the Jatilas, and they were astonished and thought: 'Has the great Sakyamuni placed himself under the spiritual direction of Kassapa, or has Kassapa become a disciple of Gotama?'   3

And the Tathāgata, reading the thoughts of the people, said to Kassapa: 'What knowledge have you gained, Kassapa, and what has induced you to renounce the sacred fire and give up your austere penances?'   4

Kassapa said: 'The profit I derived from adoring the fire was continuance in the wheel of individuality with all its sorrows and vanities. This service I have cast away, and instead of continuing penances and sacrifices I have gone in quest of the highest Nirvāna. Since I have seen the light of truth, I have abandoned worshipping the fire.' 5

The Buddha, perceiving that the whole assembly was ready as a vessel to receive the doctrine, spoke the following to Bimbisāra the king: 6

'Those who know the nature of self and understand how the senses act, find no room for selfishness, and therefore they will attain peace unending. The world holds the thought of self, and from this arises false apprehension. 7

'Some say that the self endures after death, some say it perishes. Both are wrong and their error is most grievous. 8

'For if they say the self is perishable, the fruit they strive for will perish too, and at some time there will be no hereafter. Good and evil would be indifferent. This salvation from selfishness is without merit. 9

'When some, on the other hand, say the self will not perish, then in the midst of all life and death there is but one identity unborn and undying. If such is their self, then it is perfect and cannot be perfected by deeds. The lasting, imperishable self could never be changed. The self would be lord and master, and there would be no use in perfecting the perfect; moral aims and salvation would be unnecessary. 10

'But now we see the marks of joy and sorrow. Where is any constancy? If there is no permanent self that does our deeds, then there is no self; there is no actor behind our actions, no perceiver behind our perception, no lord behind our deeds. 11

'Now attend and listen: The senses meet the object and from their contact sensation is born. From that results recollection. Thus, as the sun's power through a burning-glass causes fire to appear, so through the cognizance born of sense and object, the mind originates and with it the ego, the thought of self, whom some Brahman teachers call the lord. The shoot springs from the seed; the seed is not the shoot; both are not one and the same, but successive phases in a continuous growth. Such is the birth of animated life.   12

'Those of you who are slaves of the self and toil in its service from morning until night, those of you who live in constant fear of birth,

A VOTIVE PLAQUE DEPICTING THE BUDDHIST GOD, MGON-PO.
18TH CENTURY, TIBET.

old age, sickness, and death, receive the good tidings that your cruel master exists not. 13
'Self is an error, an illusion, a dream. Open your eyes and awaken. See things as they are and you will be comforted. 14
'Those who are awake will no longer be afraid of nightmares. Those who have recognized the nature of the rope that seemed to be a serpent will cease to tremble. 15
'Those who have found there is no self will let go all the lusts and desires of egotism. 16
'The clinging to things, covetousness, and sensuality inherited from former existences, are the causes of the misery and vanity in the world. 17
'Surrender the grasping disposition of selfishness, and you will attain to that calm state of mind which conveys perfect peace, goodness and wisdom.' 18
And the Buddha made this solemn utterance: 19

'Do not deceive, do not despise
Each other, anywhere.
Do not be angry, nor should you
Secret resentment bear;
For as a mother risks her life
And watches o'er her child,
So boundless be your love to all,
So tender, kind and mild.

'Indeed cherish goodwill right and left,
All round, early and late,
And without hindrance, without stint,
From envy free and hate,
While standing, walking, sitting down,
Whate'er you have in mind,
The rule of life that's always best
Is to be loving-kind. 21

'Gifts are great, the founding of vihāras is meritorious, meditations and religious exercises pacify the heart, comprehension of the truth leads to Nirvāna, but greater than all is loving kindness. As the light of the moon is sixteen times stronger than the light of all the stars, so loving kindness is sixteen times more efficacious in liberating the heart than all other religious accomplishments taken together.   22

'This state of heart is the best in the world. Let beings remain steadfast in it while they are awake, whether they are standing, walking, sitting, or lying down.'   23

When the Enlightened One had finished his sermon, the Magadha king said to the Blessed One: 24

'In former days, Lord, when I was a prince, I cherished five wishes. I wished that I might be inaugurated as a king. This was my first wish, and it has been fulfilled. Further, I wished: Might the Holy Buddha, the Perfect One, appear on earth while I rule and might he come to my kingdom. This was my second wish and it is fulfilled now. Further I wished: Might I pay my respects to him. This was my third wish and it is fulfilled now. The fourth wish was: Might the Blessed One preach the doctrine to me, and this is fulfilled now. The greatest wish, however, was the fifth wish: Might I understand the doctrine of the Blessed One. And this wish is fulfilled too.   25

'Most glorious is the truth preached by the Tathāgata! Our Lord, the Buddha, sets up what has been overturned; he reveals what has been hidden; he points out the way to the wanderer who has gone astray; he lights a lamp in the darkness so that those who have eyes to see may see.   26

'I take my refuge in the Buddha. I take my refuge in the Dharma. I take my refuge in the Sangha.'   27

The Tathāgata, by the exercise of his virtue and by wisdom, showed his unlimited spiritual power. He subdued and harmonized all minds. He made them see and accept the truth, and throughout the kingdom the seeds of virtue were sown.   28

XVII
Sāriputta and Moggallāna

AT THAT TIME Sāriputta and Moggallāna, two Brahmans and chiefs of the followers of Sañjaya, led a religious life. They had promised each other: 'He who first attains Nirvāna shall tell the other one.' 1
Sāriputta seeing the venerable Assaji begging for alms, modestly keeping his eyes to the ground and dignified in deportment, exclaimed: 'Truly this samana has entered the right path; I will ask him in whose name he has retired from the world and what doctrine he professes.' Being addressed by Sāriputta, Assaji replied: 'I am a follower of the Buddha, the Blessed One, but being a novice I can tell you the substance only of the doctrine.' 2
Sāriputta said: 'Tell me, venerable monk, it is the substance I want.' And Assaji recited the stanza: 3

'The Buddha did the cause unfold
Of all the things that spring from causes.
And further the great sage has told
How finally all passion pauses.' 4

Having heard this stanza, Sāriputta obtained the pure and spotless eye of truth and said: 'Now I see clearly, whatsoever is subject to origination is also subject to cessation. If this is the doctrine I have reached the state to enter Nirvāna which until now has remained hidden from me.' 5
Sāriputta went to Moggallāna and told him, and both said: 'We will go to the Blessed One, that he, the Blessed One, may be our teacher.' 6
When the Buddha saw Sāriputta and Moggallāna coming from afar, he said to his disciples, 'These two monks are highly auspicious.' 7
When the two friends had taken refuge in the Buddha, the Dharma and the Sangha, the Holy One said to his other disciples: 'Sāriputta, like the first-born son of a world-ruling monarch, is well

able to assist the king as his chief follower to set the wheel of the law rolling.'   8

And the people were annoyed. Seeing that many distinguished young men of the kingdom of Magadha led a religious life under the direction of the Blessed One, they became angry and murmured: 'Gotama Sakyamuni induces fathers to leave their wives and causes families to become extinct.'   9

When they saw the bhikkhus, they reviled them, saying: 'The great Sakyamuni has come to Rājagaha subduing the minds of men.

PADMASAMBHAVA, WHO BROUGHT BUDDHISM TO TIBET,
HOLDING RITUAL IMPLEMENTS.

Who will be the next to be led astray by him?'   10
The bhikkhus told it to the Blessed One, and the Blessed One said:
'This murmuring, bhikkhus, will not last long. It will last seven
days. If they revile you, bhikkhus, answer them with these words: 11
'"It is by preaching the truth that Tathāgatas lead beings. Who will
murmur at the wise? Who will blame the virtuous? Who will
condemn self-control, righteousness, and kindness?"'   12
And the Blessed One proclaimed this verse:

> 'Commit no wrong but good deeds do
> And let your heart be pure.
> All Buddhas teach this doctrine true
> Which will forever endure.'   13

XVIII
Anāthapindika
❀

At this time there was Anāthapindika, a man of unmeasured
wealth, visiting Rājagaha. Being of a charitable disposition, he was
called 'the supporter of orphans and the friend of the poor.'   1
Hearing that the Buddha had come into the world and was stopping
in the bamboo grove near the city, he set out in the very night to
meet the Blessed One.   2
And the Blessed One saw at once the sterling quality of Anāthapindika's heart and greeted him with words of religious comfort.
They sat down together, and Anāthapindika listened to the
sweetness of the truth preached by the Blessed One. And the
Buddha said: 3
'The restless, busy nature of the world, this, I declare, is at the root of
pain. Attain that composure of mind which is resting in the peace
of immortality. Self is but a heap of composite qualities, and its
world is empty like a fantasy.   4
'Who is it that shapes our lives? Is it Iśvara, a personal creator? If

Iśvara be the maker, all living things should have silently to submit to their maker's power. They would be like vessels formed by the potter's hand; and if it were so, how would it be possible to practise virtue? If the world had been made by Iśvara there should be no such thing as sorrow, or calamity, or evil; for both pure and impure deeds must come from him. If not, there would be another cause beside him, and he would not be self-existent.   5

'Again, it is said that the Absolute has created us. But that which is absolute cannot be a cause. All things around us come from a cause as the plant comes from the seed; but how can the Absolute be the cause of all things alike? If it pervades them, then, certainly, it does not make them.   6

'Again, it is said that Self is the maker. But if self is the maker, why did it not make things pleasing? The causes of sorrow and joy are real and objective. How can they have been made by self?   7

'Again, if we adopt the argument that there is no maker, our fate is such as it is, and there is no causation, what use would there be in shaping our lives and adjusting means to an end?   8

'Therefore, we argue that all things that exist are not without cause. However, neither Iśvara, nor the Absolute, nor the Self, nor causeless chance, is the maker, but our deeds produce results both good and evil according to the law of causation.   9

'Let us, then, abandon the heresy of worshipping Iśvara and of praying to him; let us no longer lose ourselves in vain speculations of profitless subtleties; let us surrender self and all selfishness, and as all things are fixed by causation, let us practise good so that good may result from our actions.'   10

And Anāthapindika said: 'I see that you are the Buddha, the Blessed One, the Tathāgata, and I wish to open to you my whole mind. Having listened to my words advise me what I shall do.   11

'My life is full of work, and having acquired great wealth, I am surrounded with cares. Yet I enjoy my work, and apply myself to it with all diligence. Many people are in my employ and depend upon the success of my enterprises.   12

'Now, I have heard your disciples praise the bliss of the hermit and denounce the unrest of the world. "The Holy One," they say, "has given up his kingdom and his inheritance, and has found the path of righteousness, thus setting an example to all the world how to attain Nirvāna." 13

'My heart yearns to do what is right and to be a blessing to my fellow beings. Let me then ask, Must I give up my wealth, my home, and my business enterprises, and, like yourself, go into homelessness in order to attain the bliss of a religious life?' 14

And the Buddha replied: 'The bliss of a religious life is attainable by everyone who walks in the noble eightfold path. Those that cling to wealth had better cast it away than allow their hearts to be poisoned by it; but those who do not cling to wealth, and possessing riches, use them rightly, will be a blessing to their fellow beings. 15

'It is not life and wealth and power that enslave us, but the clinging to life and wealth and power. 16

'The bhikkhu who retires from the world in order to lead a life of leisure will have no gain, for a life of indolence is an abomination, and lack of energy is to be despised. 17

'The Dharma of the Tathāgata does not require a person to go into homelessness or to resign the world, unless that person feels called upon to do so; but the Dharma of the Tathāgata requires everyone to free oneself from the illusion of self, to cleanse one's heart, to give up the thirst for pleasure and lead a life of righteousness. 18

'And whatever individuals do, whether they remain in the world as artisans, merchants, and officers of the king, or retire from the world and devote themselves to a life of religious meditation, let them put their whole heart into their task; let them be diligent and energetic, and, if they are like the lotus, which, although it grows in the water, yet remains untouched by the water, if they struggle in life without cherishing envy or hatred, if they live in the world not a life of self but a life of truth, then surely joy, peace, and bliss will dwell in their minds.' 19

XIX
The Three Characteristics and the Uncreated

WHEN THE BUDDHA WAS STAYING at the Veluvana, the bamboo
grove at Rājagaha, he addressed the monks as follows: 1
'Whether Buddhas arise, monks, or whether Buddhas do not arise, it

THANGKA PAINTING. THEMES DEPICTED ARE FIXED BY
TRADITION AND BASED ON THREE PRINCIPLES: EXPRESSION,
PROPORTION AND DETAIL. TIBET.

remains a fact and the fixed and necessary constitution of being that all conformations are transitory. This fact a Buddha discovers, masters, and discloses.   2

'Whether Buddhas arise, monks, or whether Buddhas do not arise, it remains a fact and a fixed and necessary constitution of being, that all conformations are suffering. This fact a Buddha discovers, masters, and discloses.   3

'Whether Buddhas arise, monks, or whether Buddhas do not arise, it remains a fact and a fixed and necessary constitution of being, that all conformations are lacking a self. This fact a Buddha discovers, masters, and discloses.'   4

And on another occasion the Blessed One stayed at Sāvatthī in the Jetavana, the garden of Anāthapindika.   5

At that time the Blessed One edified, aroused and gladdened the monks with a religious discourse on the subject of Nirvāna. And these monks grasping the meaning, thinking it out, and accepting with their hearts the whole doctrine, listened attentively. But there was one who had some doubt left in his heart. He said: 6

'The Buddha teaches that all conformations are transient, that all conformations are subject to sorrow, that all conformations are lacking a self. How then can there be Nirvāna, a state of eternal bliss?'   7

The Blessed One replied: 8

'There is, monks, a state where there is neither earth, nor water, nor heat, nor air; neither infinity of space nor infinity of consciousness, nor nothingness, nor perception nor nonperception; neither this world nor that world, neither sun nor moon. It is the uncreated.   9

'That, monks, I term neither coming nor going nor standing; neither death nor birth. It is without stability, without change; it is the eternal which never originates and never passes away. There is the end of sorrow.   10

'It is hard to realize the essential, the truth is not easily perceived; desire is mastered by those who know and to those who see right all things are nonexistent.   11

'There is, monks, an unborn, unoriginated, uncreated, unformed. Were there not this unborn, unoriginated, uncreated, unformed, there would be no escape from the world of the born, originated, created, formed.   12

'Since, monks, there is an unborn, unoriginated, uncreated, and unformed, therefore is there an escape from the born, originated, created, formed.'   13

XX
The Buddha's Father

☸

THE BUDDHA'S NAME BECAME famous over all India and Suddhodana, his father, sent word to him saying: 'I am growing old and wish to see my son before I die. Others have had the benefit of his doctrine, but not his father nor his relatives.'   1

And the messenger said: 'World-honored Tathāgata, your father looks for your coming as the lily longs for the rising of the sun.'   2

The Blessed One consented to the request of his father and set out on his journey to Kapilavatthu. Soon the news spread in the native country of the Buddha: 'Prince Siddhattha, who wandered forth from home into homelessness to obtain enlightenment, having attained his purpose, is coming back.'   3

Suddhodana went out with his relatives and ministers to meet the prince. When the king saw Siddhattha, his son, from afar, he was struck with his beauty and dignity, and he rejoiced in his heart, but his mouth found no words to utter.   4

This, indeed, was his son; these were the features of Siddhattha. How near was the great samana to his heart, and yet what a distance lay between them! That noble muni was no longer Siddhattha, his son; he was the Buddha, the Blessed One, the Holy One, Lord of truth, and teacher of mankind.   5

Suddhodana the king, considering the religious dignity of his son, descended from his chariot and after saluting his son said: 'It is now seven years since I have seen you. How I have longed for this moment!' 6

Then the Sakyamuni took a seat opposite his father, and the king gazed eagerly at his son. He longed to call him by his name, but he dared not. 'Siddhattha,' he exclaimed silently in his heart, 'Siddhattha, come back to your aged father and be his son again!' But seeing the determination of his son, he suppressed his sentiments, and desolation overcame him. 7

Therefore the king sat face to face with his son, rejoicing in his sadness and sad in his rejoicing. Well might he be proud of his son, but his pride broke down at the idea that his great son would never be his heir. 8

'I would offer you my kingdom,' said the king, 'but if I did, you would account it but as ashes.' 9

And the Buddha said: 'I know that the king's heart is full of love and that for his son's sake he feels deep grief. But let the ties of love that bind him to the son whom he lost embrace with equal kindness all his fellow beings, and he will receive in his place a greater one than Siddhattha; he will receive the Buddha, the teacher of truth, the preacher of righteousness, and the peace of Nirvāna will enter into his heart.' 10

Suddhodana trembled with joy when he heard the melodious words of his son, the Buddha, and clasping his hands, exclaimed with tears in his eyes: 'Wonderful is this change! The overwhelming sorrow has passed away. At first my sorrowing heart was heavy, but now I reap the fruit of your great renunciation. It was right that, moved by your mighty sympathy, you should reject the pleasures of royal power and achieve your noble purpose in religious devotion. Now that you have found the path, you can preach the law of immortality to all the world that yearns for deliverance.' 11

The king returned to the palace, while the Buddha remained in the grove before the city. 12

XXI
Yasodharā
❖

ON THE NEXT MORNING the Buddha took his bowl and set out to
beg his food.   1

And the news spread abroad: 'Prince Siddhattha is going from house
to house to receive alms in the city where he used to ride in a
chariot attended by his retinue. His robe is like a red clod, and he
holds in his hand an earthen bowl.'   2

THANGKA PAINTING. THANGKAS CAN BE USED TO SUPPORT
VISUALISATION PRACTICE. TIBET.

On hearing the strange rumor, the king went in great haste and when
he met his son he exclaimed: 'Why do you disgrace me? Don't you
know that I can easily supply you and your bhikkhus with food?' 3
And the Buddha replied: 'It is the custom of my race.'   4
But the king said: 'How can this be? You are descended from kings,
and not one of them ever begged for food.'   5
'Great king,' answered the Buddha, 'you and your race may claim
descent from kings; my descent is from the Buddhas of old. They,
begging their food, lived on alms.'   6
The king made no reply, and the Blessed One continued: 'It is
customary, to make an offering of the most precious jewel to one's
father. Suffer me, therefore, to open this treasure of mine which is
the Dharma, and accept from me this gem.'   7
And the Blessed One recited the following stanza:

> 'Rise from dreams and loiter not
> Open to truth your mind.
> Practise righteousness and you
> Eternal bliss shall find.'   8

Then the king conducted the prince into the palace, and the ministers
and all the members of the royal family greeted him with great
reverence, but Yasodharā, the mother of Rāhula, did not make her
appearance. The king sent for Yasodharā, but she replied: 'Surely, if
I am deserving of any regard, Siddhattha will come and see me.'   9
The Blessed One, having greeted all his relatives and friends, asked:
'Where is Yasodharā?' And on being informed that she had refused
to come, he rose straightway and went to her apartments.   10
'I am free,' the Blessed One said to his disciples, Sāriputta and
Moggallāna, whom he had bidden to accompany him to the
princess's chamber; 'the princess, however, is not as yet free. Not
having seen me for a long time, she is exceedingly sorrowful. Unless
her grief be allowed its course her heart will break. Should she
touch the Tathāgata, the Holy One, you must not prevent her.'   11

Yasodharā sat in her room, dressed in humble garments, and her hair cut. When Prince Siddhattha entered, she was, from the abundance of her affection, like an overflowing vessel, unable to contain her love.   12

Forgetting that the man whom she loved was the Buddha, the Lord of the world, the preacher of truth, she held him by his feet and wept bitterly.   13

Remembering, however, that Suddhodana was present, she felt ashamed, and rising, seated herself reverently at a little distance. 14

The king apologized for the princess, saying: 'This arises from her deep affection, and is more than a temporary emotion. During the seven years that she has lost her husband, when she heard that Siddhattha had shaved his head, she did likewise; when she heard that he had left off the use of perfumes and ornaments, she also refused their use. Like her husband she had eaten at appointed times from an earthen bowl only. Like him she had renounced high beds with splendid coverings, and when other princes asked her in marriage, she replied that she was still his. Therefore, grant her forgiveness.'   15

And the Blessed One spoke kindly to Yasodharā, telling of her great merits inherited from former lives.   16

XXII
Rāhula
❀

MANY PEOPLE IN KAPILAVATTHU believed in the Tathāgata and took refuge in his doctrine, among them Nanda, Siddhattha's half-brother, the son of Pajāpati; Devadatta, his cousin and brother-in-law; Upāli the barber; and Anuruddha the philosopher. Some years later Ānanda, another cousin of the Blessed One, also joined the Sangha.   1

Ānanda was a man after the heart of the Blessed One; he was his most beloved disciple, profound in comprehension and gentle in spirit.

And Ānanda remained always near the Blessed Master of truth, until death parted them.   2

On the seventh day after the Buddha's arrival in Kapilavatthu, Yasodharā dressed Rāhula, now seven years old, in all the splendor of a prince and said to him: 3

'This holy man, whose appearance is so glorious that he looks like the great Brahmā, is your father. He possesses four great mines of wealth which I have not yet seen. Go to him and entreat him to put you in possession of them, for the son ought to inherit the property of his father.'   4

Rāhula replied: 'I know of no father but the king. Who is my father?'   5

The princess took the boy in her arms and from the window she pointed out to him the Buddha, who happened to be near the palace, partaking of food.   6

Rāhula then went to the Buddha, and looking up into his face said without fear and with much affection: 'My father!'   7

And standing near him, he added: 'O samana, even your shadow is a place of bliss!'   8

When the Tathāgata had finished his meal, he gave blessings and went away from the palace, but Rāhula followed and asked his father for his inheritance.   9

No one prevented the boy, nor did the Blessed One himself.   10

Then the Blessed One turned to Sāriputta, saying: 'My son asks for his inheritance. I cannot give him perishable treasures that will bring cares and sorrows, but I can give him the inheritance of a holy life, which is a treasure that will not perish.'   11

Addressing Rāhula with earnestness, the Blessed One said: 'Gold and silver and jewels are not in my possession. But if you are willing to receive spiritual treasures, and are strong enough to carry them and to keep them, I shall give you the four truths which will teach you the eightfold path of righteousness. Do you desire to be admitted to the brotherhood of those who devote their life to the culture of the heart seeking for the highest bliss attainable?'   12

And Rāhula replied with firmness: 'I do. I want to join the brotherhood of the Buddha.' 13

When the king heard that Rāhula had joined the order of bhikkhus he was grieved. He had lost Siddhattha and Nanda, his sons, and Devadatta, his nephew. But now that his grandson had been taken from him, he went to the Blessed One and spoke to him. And the Blessed One promised that from that time forward he would not ordain any minor without the consent of his parents or guardians. 14

SEATED FIGURE, WITH HANDS RAISED IN A GESTURE OF
TEACHING. TIBET.

CONSOLIDATION
OF THE BUDDHA'S RELIGION

XXIII
Women Admitted to the Sangha
*

YASODHARĀ HAD THREE TIMES requested of the Buddha that she might be admitted to the Sangha, but her wish had not been granted. Now Pajāpatī, the foster mother of the Blessed One, in the company of Yasodharā, and many other women, went to the Tathāgata entreating him earnestly to let them take the vows and be ordained as disciples. 1

And the Blessed One, foreseeing the danger that lurked in admitting women to the Sangha, protested that while the good religion ought surely to last a thousand years it would, when women joined it, likely decay after five hundred years; but observing the zeal of Pajāpatī and Yasodharā for leading a religious life he could no longer resist and assented to have them admitted as his disciples. 2

Then the venerable Ānanda addressed the Blessed One as follows: 3

'Are women competent, Venerable Lord, if they retire from household life to the homeless state, under the doctrine and discipline announced by the Tathāgata, to attain to the fruit of conversion, to attain to a release from a wearisome repetition of rebirths, to attain to Arahatship?' 4

And the Blessed One declared: 'Women are so competent, Ānanda.' 5

Pajāpatī was the first woman to become a disciple of the Buddha and to receive the ordination as a bhikkhunī. 6

XXIV
The Bhikkhus' Conduct toward Women
*

THE BHIKKHUS CAME to the Blessed One and asked him: 1

'Lord what conduct toward women do you prescribe to the samanas who have left the world?' 2

STORE: 0120   REG: 08/79   TRAN#: 2789
SALE   05/25/2000 EMP: 02158

TEACHINGS OF BUDDHA
5708320 CL T   12.95
PERIODICAL
FR N   3.99

Subtotal   16.94
MASSACHUSETTS 5%   .65
2 Items   Total   17.59
CASH   20.10
CASH   2.51-

05/25/2000 04:10PM

- Merchandise must be in salable condition
- Opened videos, discs, and cassettes may be exchanged for replacement copies of the original item only
- Periodicals and newspapers may not be returned
- Items purchased by check may be returned for cash after 10 business days.
- All returned checks will incur a $15 service charge

BORDERS®

- Returns must be accompanied by receipt
- Returns must be completed within 30 days
- Merchandise must be in salable condition
- Opened videos, discs, and cassettes may be exchanged for replacement copies of the original item only
- Periodicals and newspapers may not be returned
- Items purchased by check may be returned for cash after 10 business days.
- All returned checks will incur a $15 service charge

BORDERS®

- Returns must be accompanied by receipt
- Returns must be completed within 30 days
- Merchandise must be in salable condition
- Opened videos, discs, and cassettes may be exchanged for replacement copies of the original item only
- Periodicals and newspapers may not be returned
- Items purchased by check may be returned for cash after 10 business days.

And the Blessed One said: 3

'Guard against looking on a woman. 4

'If you see a woman, let it be as though you saw her not, and have no conversation with her. 5

'If, after all, you must speak with her, let it be with a pure heart, and think to yourself, "I as a samana will live in this world as the spotless leaf of the lotus, unsoiled by the mud in which it grows." 6

'If the woman is old, regard her as your mother, if young, as your sister, if very young, as your child. 7

'The samana who looks on a woman as a woman, or touches her as a woman, has broken his vow and is no longer a disciple of the Tathāgata. 8

'The power of lust is great with men, and is to be feared; take then the bow of earnest perseverance, and the sharp arrows of wisdom. 9

'Cover your heads with the helmet of right thought, and fight with fixed resolve against the five desires. 10

'Lust beclouds a man's heart, when it is confused with woman's beauty, and the mind is dazed. 11

'Better far with red-hot irons bore out both your eyes, than encourage in yourself sensual thoughts, or look upon a woman's form with lustful desires. 12

'Better fall into the fierce tiger's mouth, or under the sharp knife of the executioner, than dwell with a woman and excite in yourself lustful thoughts. 13

'A woman of the world is anxious to exhibit her form and shape, whether walking, standing, sitting, or sleeping. Even when represented as a picture, she desires to captivate with the charms of her beauty, and thus to rob men of their steadfast heart. 14

'How then ought you to guard yourselves? 15

'By regarding her tears and her smiles as enemies, her stooping form, her hanging arms, and her disentangled hair as toils designed to entrap man's heart. 16

'Therefore, I say, restrain the heart, give it no unbridled license.' 17

XXV
Devadatta

*

WHEN DEVADATTA, THE SON of Suprabuddha and a brother of Yasodharā, became a disciple, he cherished the hope of attaining the same distinctions and honors as Gotama Siddhattha. Being disappointed in his ambitions, he conceived in his heart a jealous hatred, and, attempting to excel the Perfect One in virtue, he found fault with his regulations and reproved them as too lenient.   1

Devadatta went to Rājagaha and gained the ear of Ajātasattu, the son of King Bimbisāra. And Ajātasattu built a new vihāra for Devadatta, and founded a sect whose disciples were pledged to severe rules and self-mortification.   2

Soon afterwards the Blessed One himself came to Rājagaha and stayed at the Veluvana vihāra.   3

Devadatta called on the Blessed One, requesting him to sanction his rules of greater stringency, by which a greater holiness might be procured. 'The body,' he said, 'consists of its thirty-two parts and has no divine attributes. It is born in corruption. Its attributes are liability to pain and dissolution, for it is impermanent. It is the receptacle of karma which is the curse of our former existences; it is the dwelling place of defilements and diseases and its organs constantly discharge disgusting secretions. Its end is death and its goal the charnel house. Such being the condition of the body it is incumbent upon us to treat it as a carcass full of abomination and to clothe it in such rags only as have been gathered in cemeteries or upon dung hills.'   4

The Blessed One said: 'Truly, the body is full of impurity and its end is the charnel house, for it is impermanent and destined to be dissolved into its elements. But being the receptacle of karma, it lies in our power to make it a vessel of truth and not of evil. It is not good to indulge in the pleasures of the body, but neither is it good to neglect our bodily needs and to heap filth upon impurities. The lamp that is not cleansed and not filled with oil will be extinguished, and a body that is unkempt, unwashed, and weakened by penance will not be a fit receptacle for the light of truth. Attend to your body and its needs as you would treat a wound which you care for without loving it. Severe rules will not lead the disciples on the middle path which I have taught. Certainly, no one can be prevented from keeping more stringent rules, if a person sees fit to do so, but they should not be imposed upon anyone, for they are unnecessary.'   5

PORCELAIN BUDDHA. CH'IEN LUNG PERIOD, CHINA.

Thus the Tathāgata refused Devadatta's proposal and Devadatta left the Buddha and went into the vihāra speaking evil of the Lord's path of salvation as too lenient and altogether insufficient.   6

When the Blessed One heard of Devadatta's intrigues, he said: 'Among men there is no one who is not blamed. People blame one who sits silent and one who speaks, they also blame one who preaches the middle path.'   7

Devadatta instigated Ajātasattu to plot against his father Bimbisāra, the king, so that the prince would no longer be subject to him; Bimbisāra was imprisoned by his son in a tower where he died leaving the kingdom of Magadha to his son Ajātasattu.   8

The new king listened to the evil advice of Devadatta, and he gave orders to take the life of the Tathāgata. However, the murderers sent out to kill the Lord could not perform their vile deed, and became converted as soon as they saw him and listened to his preaching. The rock hurled down from a precipice upon the great Master split in two, and the pieces passed by on either side without doing any harm. Nalagiri, the wild elephant let loose to destroy the Lord, became gentle in his presence, and Ajātasattu, suffering greatly from the pangs of his conscience, went to the Blessed One and sought peace in his distress.   9

The Blessed One received Ajātasattu kindly and taught him the way of salvation, but Devadatta still tried to become the founder of a religious school of his own.   10

Devadatta did not succeed in his plans and having been abandoned by many of his disciples, he fell sick, and then repented. He entreated those who had remained with him to carry his litter to the Buddha, saying: 'Take me to him; though I have done evil to him, I am his brother-in-law. For the sake of our relationship the Buddha will save me.' And they obeyed, although reluctantly.   11

And Devadatta in his impatience to see the Blessed One rose from his litter while his carriers were washing their hands. But his feet burned under him, he sank to the ground, and, having chanted a hymn on the Buddha, died.   12

XXVI
Name and Form
*

ON ONE OCCASION the Blessed One entered the assembly hall and
the monks hushed their conversation.   1

When they had greeted him with clasped hands, they sat down and
became composed. Then the Blessed One said: 'Your minds are
inflamed with intense interest; what was the topic of your
discussion?'   2

Sāriputta rose and said: 'World-honored master, we were discussing
the nature of a person's own existence. We were trying to grasp
the mixture of our own being which is called Name and Form.
Every human being consists of conformations, and there are three
groups which are not corporeal. They are sensation, perception,
and the dispositions, all three constitute consciousness and mind,
being comprised under the term Name. And there are four elements
– the earthy element, the watery element, the fiery element, and the
gaseous element – and these four elements constitute a person's
bodily form, being held together so that this machine moves
like a puppet. How does this name and form endure and how
can it live?'   3

The Blessed One said: 'Life is instantaneous and living is dying. Just as
a chariot-wheel in rolling rolls only at one point of the tire, and in
resting rests only at one point; in exactly the same way, the life of a
living being lasts only for the period of one thought. As soon as that
thought has ceased, the being is said to have ceased.   4

'As it has been said:– "The being of a past moment of thought has
lived, but does not live, nor will it live. The being of a future
moment of thought will live, but has not lived, nor does it live. The
being of the present moment of thought does live, but has not
lived, nor will it live."'   5

'As to Name and Form we must understand how they interact. Name
has no power of its own, nor can it go on of its own impulse, either
to eat, or to drink, or to utter sounds, or to make a movement.

Form also is without power and cannot go on of its own impulse. It has no desire to eat, or to drink, or to utter sounds, or to make a movement. But Form goes on when supported by Name, and Name when supported by Form. When Name has a desire to eat, or to drink, or to utter sounds, or to make a movement, then Form eats, drinks, utters sounds, makes a movement.   6

'It is as if two men, the one blind from birth and the other a cripple, were desirous of going traveling, and the man blind from birth were to say to the cripple as follows: "See here! I am able to use my legs, but I have no eyes with which to see the rough and the smooth places in the road."   7

'And the cripple were to say: "See here! I am able to use my eyes, but I have no legs with which to go forward and back."   8

'And the blind man, pleased and delighted, were to lift the cripple onto his shoulders. And the cripple sitting on the shoulders of the blind man were to direct him, saying, "Leave the left and go to the right; leave the right and go to the left."   9

'Here the man blind from birth is without power of his own, and weak, and cannot go of his own impulse or might. The cripple also is without power of his own, and weak, and cannot go of his own impulse or might. Yet when they mutually support one another it is not impossible for them to go.   10

'In exactly the same way, Name is without power of its own, and cannot spring up of its own might, nor perform this or that action. Form also is without power of its own, and cannot spring up of its own might, nor perform this or that action. Yet when they mutually support one another it is not impossible for them to spring up and go on.   11

'There is no material that exists for the production of Name and Form; and when Name and Form cease, they do not go anywhere in space. After Name and Form have ceased, they do not exist anywhere in the shape of heaped up music material. Thus when a lute is played upon, there is no previous store of sound; and when the music ceases it does not go anywhere in space. When it has ceased, it exists nowhere in a stored up state. Having previously been nonexistent, it came into existence on account of the structure and stem of the lute and the exertions of the performer, and as it came into existence so it passes away. In exactly the same way, all the elements of being, both corporeal and noncorporeal come into existence after having previously been nonexistent; and having come into existence pass away.   12

'There is not a self residing in Name and Form, but the cooperation of the conformations produces what people call a person.   13

'Just as the word "chariot" is but a mode of expression for axle, wheels, the chariot-body and other constituents in their proper combination, so a living being is the appearance of the groups with

SHAKYAMUNI BUDDHA, THE HISTORICAL FOUNDER OF
BUDDHISM. 19TH CENTURY, TIBET.

the four elements as they are joined in a unit. There is no self in the
carriage and there is no self in a being.   14

'Bhikkhus, this doctrine is sure and an eternal truth, that there is no
self outside of its parts. This self of ours which constitutes Name
and Form is a combination of the groups with the four elements,
but there is no ego entity, no self in itself.   15

'Paradoxical though it may sound: There is a path to walk on, there is
walking being done, but there is no traveler. There are deeds being
done, but there is no doer. There is a blowing of the air, but there is
no wind that does the blowing. The thought of self is an error and
all existences are as hollow as the plantain tree and as empty as
twirling water bubbles.   16

'Therefore, bhikkhus, as there is no self, there is no transmigration
of a self; but there are deeds and the continued effect of deeds.
There is a rebirth of karma. This rebirth, this reappearance of the
conformations is continuous and depends on the law of cause
and effect. Just as a seal is impressed upon the wax reproducing
the configurations of its device, so the thoughts of beings,
their characters, their aspirations are impressed upon others
in continuous transference and continue their karma, and good
deeds will continue in blessings while bad deeds will continue
in curses.   17

'There is no entity here that migrates, no self is transferred from one
place to another; but there is a voice uttered here and the echo of it
comes back. The teacher pronounces a stanza and the disciple who
attentively listens to the teacher's instruction, repeats the stanza.
Thus the stanza is reborn in the mind of the disciple.   18

'The body is a compound of perishable organs. It is subject to decay,
and we should take care of it as of a wound or a sore; we should
attend to its needs without being attached to it, or loving it.   19

'The body is like a machine, and there is no self in it that makes it
walk or act, but the thoughts of it, as the windy elements, cause the
machine to work.   20

'The body moves about like a cart. Therefore it is said: 21

'As ships are by the wind impelled,
As arrows from their bowstrings speed,
So likewise when the body moves
The windy element must lead.   22
'Machines are geared to work by ropes;
So too this body is, in fact,
Directed by a mental pull
Whene'er it stand or sit or act.   23

'No independent self is here
That could intrinsic forces prove
To make people act without a cause,
To make them stand or walk or move.   24

'Only those who utterly abandon all thought of the ego escape the
snares of the Evil One; they are out of the reach of Māra.   25
'Thus says the pleasure-promising tempter: 26

'So long as to the things
Called "mine" and "I" and "me"
Your anxious heart still clings,
My snares you cannot flee.'   27

'The faithful disciple replies: 28

'Naught's mine and naught of me,
The self I do not mind!
Thus Māra, I tell you,
My path you cannot find.'   29

'Dismiss the error of the self and do not cling to possessions which
are transient but perform deeds that are good, for deeds are
enduring and in deeds your karma continues.   30
'Since then, bhikkhus, there is no self, there cannot be any afterlife of

a self. Therefore abandon all thought of self. But since there are
deeds and since deeds continue, be careful with your deeds.   31
'All beings have karma as their portion: they are heirs of their karma;
they are sprung from their karma; their karma is their kinsman;
their karma is their refuge; karma allots beings to meanness or to
greatness.   32

'Assailed by death in life's throes
On quitting all your joys and woes
What is your own, your recompense?
What stays with you when passing hence?
What like a shadow follows you
And will Beyond your heirloom be?

'Tis deeds, your deeds, both good and bad;
Naught else can after death be had.
Your deeds are yours, your recompense;
They are your own when going hence;
They like a shadow follow you
And will Beyond your heirloom be.

'Let all then here perform good deeds,
For future wealth a treasure store;
There to reap crops from noble seeds,
A bliss increasing evermore.'   35

XXVII
THE VANITY OF WORLDLINESS
*

THERE WAS A POET who had acquired the spotless eye of truth, and
he believed in the Buddha, whose doctrine gave him peace of mind
and comfort in the hour of affliction.   1
And it happened that an epidemic swept over the country in which

he lived, so that many died, and the people were terrified. Some of them trembled with fright, and in anticipation of their fate were overwhelmed with all the horrors of death before they died, while others began to be merry, shouting loudly, 'Let us enjoy ourselves today, for we do not know whether tomorrow we shall live'; yet their laughter was no genuine gladness, but a mere pretence and affectation.   2

Among all these worldly men and women trembling with anxiety, the Buddhist poet lived in the time of the pestilence, as usual, calm and

BUDDHIST SAGE. TOSA SCHOOL, 15TH CENTURY.

undisturbed, helping wherever he could and ministering to the sick, soothing their pains by medicine and religious consolation   3

And a man came to him and said: 'My heart is nervous and excited, for I see people die. I am not anxious about others, but I tremble because of myself. Help me: cure me of my fear.'   4

The poet replied: 'There is help for those who have compassion on others, but there is no help for you so long as you cling to your own self alone. Hard times try the souls of beings and teach them righteousness and charity. Can you witness these sad sights around you and still be filled with selfishness? Can you see your brothers, sisters, and friends suffer, yet not forget the petty cravings and lust of your own heart?'   5

Noticing the desolation in the mind of the pleasure-seeking man, the Buddhist poet composed this song and taught it to the brethren in the vihāra: 6

'Unless refuge you take in the Buddha
    and find in Nirvāna rest
Your life is but vanity – empty and desolate vanity.
To see the world is idle, and to enjoy life is empty.
The world, including mankind, is but like a phantom,
    and the hope of heaven is as a mirage.   7

'Worldlings seek pleasures fattening themselves
    like caged fowl.
But the Buddhist sage flies up to the sun like the wild crane.
The fowl in the coop has food but will soon
    be boiled in the pot.
No provisions are given to the wild crane,
    but the heavens and the earth are his.'   8

The poet said: 'The times are hard and teach the people a lesson; yet they do not heed it.' And he composed another poem on the vanity of worldliness: 9

'It is good to reform, and it is good to exhort people to reform.
The things of the world will all be swept away.
Let others be busy and buried with care.
My mind all unvexed shall be pure.   10

'After pleasures they hanker and find no satisfaction;
Riches they covet and can never have enough.
They are like puppets held up by a string.
When the string breaks they come down with a shock.   11

'In the domain of death there are neither great nor small;
Neither gold nor silver is used, nor precious jewels.
No distinction is made between the high and the low.
And daily the dead are buried beneath the fragrant sod.   12

'Look at the sun setting behind the western hills.
You lie down to rest, but soon the cock will announce morn.
Reform today and do not wait until it is too late.
Do not say it is early, for the time quickly passes by.   13

'It is good to reform and it is good to exhort people to reform.
It is good to lead a righteous life and take refuge
   in the Buddha's name.
Your talents may reach to the skies,
   your wealth may be untold –
But all is in vain unless you attain the peace of Nirvāna.'   14

XXVIII
The Annihilation of Suffering
*

AND THE BUDDHA SAID: 'What, my friends, is evil?   1
'Killing is evil; stealing is evil; yielding to sexual passion is evil; lying
is evil; slandering is evil; abuse is evil; gossip is evil; envy is evil;

hatred is evil; to cling to false doctrine is evil; all these things, my friends, are evil. 2

'And what, my friends, is the root of evil? 3

'Desire is the root of evil; hatred is the root of evil; illusion is the root of evil; these things are the root of evil. 4

'What, however, is good? 5

'Abstaining from killing is good; abstaining from theft is good; abstaining from sensuality is good; abstaining from falsehood is good; abstaining from slander is good; suppression of unkindness is good; abandoning gossip is good; letting go all envy is good; dismissing hatred is good; obedience to the truth is good; all these things are good. 7

'Freedom from desire is the root of the good; freedom from hatred and freedom from illusion; these things, my friends, are the root of the good. 8

'What, however, is suffering? What is the origin of suffering? What is the annihilation of suffering? 9

'Birth is suffering; old age is suffering; disease is suffering; death is suffering; sorrow and misery are suffering; affliction and despair are suffering; to be united with loathsome things is suffering; the loss of that which we love and the failure in attaining that which is longed for are suffering; all these things are suffering. 10

'And what is the origin of suffering? 11

'It is lust, passion, and the thirst for existence that yearns for pleasure everywhere, leading to a continual rebirth! It is sensuality, desire, selfishness; all these things, are the origin of suffering. 12

'And what is the annihilation of suffering? 13

'The radical and total annihilation of this thirst and the abandonment, the liberation, the deliverance from passion, that is the annihilation of suffering. 14

'And what is the path that leads to the annihilation of suffering? 15

'It is the holy eightfold path that leads to the annihilation of suffering, which consists of, right views, right thought, right speech, right action, right living, right effort, right mindfulness, and right concentration.   16

'In so far as a noble youth recognizes suffering and the origin of
suffering, as that young person recognizes the annihilation of
suffering, and walks on the path that leads to the annihilation of
suffering, radically forsaking passion, subduing anger, annihilating
the vain conceit of the "I-am," leaving ignorance, and attaining to
enlightenment, that person will make an end of all suffering even
in this life.'   17

XXIX
Avoiding the Ten Evils

THE BUDDHA SAID: 'All acts of living creatures become bad by ten
things, and by avoiding the ten things they become good. There are
three evils of the body, four evils of the tongue, and three evils of
the mind.   1

'The evils of the body are, murder, theft, and adultery; of the tongue,
lying, slander, abuse, and idle talk; of the mind, covetousness,
hatred, and error.   2

'I urge you to avoid the ten evils: 3

    'I. Do not kill, but have regard for life.   4

    'II. Do not steal; but help everybody to be master of the
    fruits of their labors.   5

    'III. Abstain from impurity, and lead a life of chastity.   6

    'IV. Do not lie, but be truthful. Speak the truth with
    discretion, fearlessly and in a loving heart.   7

    'V. Do not invent evil reports, nor repeat them. Do not
    find fault, but look for the good sides of your fellow
    beings, so that you may with sincerity defend them
    against their enemies.   8

    'VI. Do not swear, but speak decently and with dignity.   9

    'VII. Do not waste time with gossip, but speak to the
    purpose or keep silence.   10

'VIII. Do not covet, nor envy, but rejoice at the fortunes of other people.   11

'IX. Cleanse your heart of malice and cherish no hatred, not even against your enemies; but embrace all living beings with kindness.   12

'X. Free your mind of ignorance and be anxious to learn the truth, especially in the one thing that is needful, in case you fall a prey either to scepticism or to errors. Scepticism will make you indifferent and errors will lead you astray, so that you shall not find the noble path that leads to life eternal.'   13

MANJUSRI, THE BODHISATTVA OF WISDOM.
18TH CENTURY, TIBET.

THE TEACHER

XXX
The Dhammapada
✳

THIS IS THE PATH OF TRUTH pursued by those who are followers of
the Buddha: 1

Creatures from mind their character derive; mind-marshalled are they,
mind-made. Mind is the source either of bliss or of corruption. 2

By oneself evil is done; by oneself one suffers; by oneself evil is left
undone; by oneself one is purified. Purity and impurity belong to
oneself, no one can purify another. 3

You yourself must make an effort. Tathāgatas only point the way.
The thoughtful who enter the way are freed from the bondage of
Māra. 4

Those who do not rouse themselves when it is time to rise; who,
though young and strong, are full of sloth; whose will and thoughts
are weak; those lazy and idle people will never find the way to
enlightenment. 5

If you hold yourself dear, watch yourself carefully; the truth guards
those who guard themselves. 6

If you make yourself as you teach others to be, then, being yourself
subdued, you may subdue others; one's own self is indeed difficult
to subdue. 7

If some men conquer in battle a thousand times a thousand men, and
if another conquer himself, he is the greatest of conquerors. 8

It is the habit of fools, be they laymen or members of the order, to
think, 'this is done by me. May others be subject to me. In this or that
transaction a prominent part should be played by me.' Fools do not
care for the duty to be performed or the aim to be reached, but think
of their self alone. Everything is but a pedestal of their vanity. 9

Bad deeds, and deeds hurtful to ourselves, are easy to do; what is beneficial and good, that is very difficult. 10

If anything is to be done, let a person do it, let a person attack it vigorously! 11

Before long, alas! this body will lie on the earth, despised, without understanding, like a useless log; yet our thoughts will endure. They will be thought again, and will produce action. Good thoughts will produce good actions, and bad thoughts will produce bad actions. 12

Earnestness is the path of immortality, thoughtlessness the path of death. Those who are in earnest do not die; those who are thoughtless are as if dead already. 13

Those who imagine they find truth in untruth, and see untruth in truth, will never arrive at truth, but follow vain desires. They who know truth in truth, and untruth in untruth, arrive at truth, and follow true desires. 14

As rain breaks through an ill-thatched house, passion will break through an unreflecting mind. As rain does not break through a well-thatched house, passion will not break through a well-reflecting mind. 15

Well makers lead the water wherever they like; fletchets bend the arrow; carpenters bend a log of wood; wise people fashion themselves; wise people falter not amidst blame and praise. Having listened to the law, they become serene, like a deep, smooth, and still lake. 16

If one speaks or acts with an evil thought, pain follows one as the wheel follows the foot of the ox that draws the carriage. 17

An evil deed is better left undone, for one will repent of it afterwards; a good deed is better done, for having done it one will not repent. 18

If a wrong is committed let it not be done again; let there be no delight in wrongdoing; pain is the outcome of evil. If good is done, let it be done again; let there be delight in it; happiness is the outcome of good. 19

Let no one think lightly of evil, saying 'It will not come near me.' As

by the falling of water drops a water pot is filled, so the fool
becomes full of evil, though it is gathered little by little.   20

Let no one think lightly of good, saying 'It will not come near me.' As
by the falling of water drops a water pot is filled, so the wise
become full of good, though they gather it little by little.   21

Those who live for pleasure only, whose senses are uncontrolled,
immoderate in their food, idle, and weak, them Māra, the tempter,
will certainly overthrow, as the wind throws down a weak tree.
Those who live without looking for pleasures, whose senses are well

IVORY FIGURE OF THE BUDDHA ON A TURQUOISE MATRIX
THRONE. MING DYNASTY, CHINA.

controlled, moderate in their food, faithful and strong, them Māra will certainly not overthrow, any more than the wind throws down a rocky mountain. 22

The fool who knows his or her foolishness, is wise at least so far. But a fool who thinks himself or herself wise, is a fool indeed. 23

To evildoers wrong appears sweet as honey; they look upon it as pleasant so long as it bears no fruit; but when its fruit ripens, then they look upon it as wrong. And so the good look upon the goodness of the Dharma as a burden and an evil so long as it bears no fruit; but when its fruit ripens, then its goodness is seen. 24

A hater may do great harm to a hater, or an enemy to an enemy; but a wrongly directed mind will do greater mischief to itself. A mother, a father, or any other relative will do much good; but a well directed mind will do greater service to itself. 25

Those whose evil is very great bring themselves down to that state where their enemies wish them to be. They themselves are their greatest enemy. Thus a creeper destroys the life of a tree on which it finds support. 26

Do not direct your thought to what gives pleasure, that you may not cry out when burning, 'This is pain.' The evil burn by their own deeds, as if burnt by fire. 27

Pleasures destroy the foolish; the foolish by their thirst for pleasures destroy themselves as if they were their own enemy. The fields are damaged by hurricanes and weeds; mankind is damaged by passion, by hatred, by vanity, and by lust. 28

Let no one ever take into consideration whether a thing is pleasant or unpleasant. The love of pleasure brings grief and the dread of pain causes fear; those who are free from the love of pleasure and the dread of pain know neither grief nor fear. 29

Those who give themselves to vanity, and do not give themselves to meditation, forgetting the real aim of life and grasping at pleasure, will in time envy those who have exerted themselves in meditation. 30

The fault of others is easily noticed, but that of oneself is difficult to perceive. Like chaff one winnows other's faults but hides his own, as a cheat hides the false dice from the gambler.　31

If one looks after the faults of others, and is always inclined to take offence, one's own passions will grow, and one is far from the destruction of passions.　32

Not about the perversities of others, not about their sins of commission or omission, but about one's own misdeeds and negligences alone should a sage be worried.　33

Good people shine from afar, like the snowy mountains; bad people are concealed, like arrows shot by night.　34

If people by causing pain to others, wish to obtain pleasure for themselves, they, entangled in the bonds of selfishness, will never be free from hatred.　35

Let a person overcome anger by love, overcome evil by good, overcome the greedy by liberality, the liar by truth!　36

For hatred does not cease by hatred at any time; hatred ceases by nonhatred, this is an old rule.　37

Speak the truth; do not yield to anger; give, if you are asked. By these three steps you will become divine.　38

Let the wise blow off the impurities of their selves, as a smith blows off the impurities of silver, one by one, little by little, and from time to time.　39

Lead others, not by violence, but by righteousness and equity.　40

Those who possess virtue and intelligence, who are just, speak the truth, and do what is their own business, those people the world will hold dear.　41

As the bee collects nectar and departs without injuring the flower, or its color or scent, so let a sage dwell in the community.　42

If a traveller does not meet one who is better, or equal, let that person firmly keep to a solitary journey; there is no companionship with fools.　43

Long is the night to those who are awake; long is a mile to those who are tired; long is life to the foolish who do not know the true law.　44

Better than living a hundred years, not seeing the highest truth, is a
day in the life of one who sees the highest truth.   45
Some form their Dharma arbitrarily and fabricate it artificially; they
advance complex speculations and imagine that good results are
attainable only by the acceptance of their theories; yet the truth is
but one; there are not different truths in the world. Having reflected
on the various theories, we have gone into the yoke with one who
has shaken off all sin. But shall we be able to proceed together.   46
The best of ways is the eightfold path. This is the path. There is no
other that leads to the purifying of intelligence. Go on this path!
Everything else is the deceit of Māra, the tempter. If you go on this
path, you will make an end of pain! The Tathāgata says, The path
was preached by me, when I had understood the removal of the
thorn in the flesh.   47
Not only by discipline and vows, not only by much learning, do
I earn the happiness of release which no worldling can know.
Bhikkhu, be not confident as long as you have not attained the
extinction of thirst. The extinction of evil desire is the highest truth. 48
The gift of the dharma exceeds all gifts; the sweetness of dharma
exceeds all sweetness; the delight in dharma exceeds all delights; the
extinction of thirst overcomes all pain.   49
Few are there who cross the river and reach the goal. The great
multitudes are running up and down the shore; but there is no
suffering for those who have finished their journey.   50
As the lily will grow full of sweet perfume and delight upon a heap of
rubbish, so the disciple of the truly enlightened Buddha shines
forth by wisdom among those who walk in darkness.   51
Let us live happily then, not hating those who hate us! Among those
who hate us let us dwell free from hatred!   52
Let us live happily then, free from all ailments among the ailing!
Among those who are ailing let us dwell free from ailments!   53
Let us live happily, then, free from greed among the greedy! Among
those who are greedy let us dwell free from greed!   54
The sun is bright by day, the moon shines by night, the warrior is

bright in his armor, the Brahmin is bright in meditation; but among all the brightest with splendor day and night is the Buddha, the Awakened, the Holy, Blessed. 55

XXXI
Identity and Nonidentity
❉

KŪTADANTA, THE HEAD OF THE BRAHMANS in the village of Dānamatī having approached the Blessed One respectfully, greeted him and said: 'I am told, samana, that you are the Buddha, the Holy One, the All Knowing, the Lord of the world. But if you were the Buddha, would you not come like a king in all your glory and power?' 1

The Blessed One said: 'Your eyes are dim. If the eye of your mind were

AVALOKITESHVARA, THE BODHISATTVA OF COMPASSION, SHOWING 11 FACES AND 1000 ARMS. TIBET.

bright you could see the glory and the power of truth.'   2

Kūtadanta said: 'Show me the truth and I shall see it. But your
doctrine is without consistency. If it were consistent, it would stand,
but as it is not, it will pass away.'   3

The Blessed One replied: 'The truth will never pass away.'   4

Kūtadanta said: 'I am told that you teach the law, yet you tear down
religion. Your disciples despise rites and abandon immolation, but
reverence for the gods can be shown only by sacrifices. The very
nature of religion consists in worship and sacrifice.'   5

The Buddha said: 'Greater than the immolation of bullocks is the
sacrifice of self. One who offers to the gods evil desires will see the
uselessness of slaughtering animals at the altar. Blood has no cleansing
power, but the eradication of lust will make the heart pure. Better than
worshipping gods is obedience to the laws of righteousness.'   6

Kūtadanta, being of a religious disposition and anxious about his fate
after death, had sacrificed countless victims. Now he saw the folly
of atonement by blood. Not yet satisfied, however, with the
teachings of the Tathāgata, Kūtadanta continued: 'You believe,
Master, that beings are reborn, that they migrate in the evolution of
life, and that subject to the law of karma we must reap what we sow.
Yet you teach the nonexistence of the soul! Your disciples praise
utter self-extinction as the highest bliss of Nirvāna. If I am merely a
combination of the sankhāras, my existence will cease when I die.
If I am merely a compound of sensations and ideas and desires, to
what place can I go at the dissolution of the body?'   7

The Blessed One said: 'Brahman, you are religious and earnest. You
are seriously concerned about your soul. Yet your work is in vain
because you are lacking in the one thing that is needful.   8

'There is rebirth of character, but no transmigration of a self. Your
thought-forms reappear, but there is no ego-entity transferred. The
stanza uttered by a teacher is reborn in the scholar who repeats
the words.   9

'Only through ignorance and delusion do people indulge in the
dream that their souls are separate and self-existent entities.   10

'Your heart, Brahman, is still clinging to self; you are anxious about heaven but you seek the pleasures of self in heaven, and so you cannot see the bliss of truth and the immortality of truth.   11

'I say to you: The Blessed One has not come to teach death, but to teach life, and you do not discern the nature of living and dying. 12

'This body will be dissolved and no amount of sacrifice will save it. Therefore, seek the life that is of the mind. Where self is, truth cannot be; yet when truth comes, self will disappear. Therefore, let your mind rest in the truth; propagate the truth, put your whole will in it, and let is spread. In the truth you shall live forever.   13

'Self is death and truth is life. The clinging to self is a perpetual dying, while moving in the truth is partaking of Nirvāna which is life everlasting.'   14

Kūtadanta said: 'Where, venerable Master, is Nirvāna?'   15

'Nirvāna is wherever the precepts are obeyed,' replied the Blessed One. 16

'Do I understand you rightly,' continued the Brahman, 'that Nirvāna is not a place, and being nowhere it is without reality?'   17

'You do not understand me rightly,' said the Blessed One. 'Now listen and answer these questions: Where does the wind dwell?'   18

'Nowhere,' was the reply.   19

Buddha continued: 'Then, sir, there is no such thing as wind.'   20

Kūtadanta made no reply; and the Blessed One asked again: 'Answer me, Brahman, where does wisdom dwell? Is wisdom a locality?'   21

'Wisdom has no allotted dwelling place,' replied Kūtadanta.   22

The Blessed One said: 'Do you mean that there is no wisdom, no enlightenment, no righteousness, and no salvation, because Nirvāna is not a locality? As a great and mighty wind which passes over the world in the heat of the day, so the Tathāgata comes to blow over the minds of mankind with the breath of love, so cool, so sweet, so calm, so delicate; and those tormented by fever assuage their suffering and rejoice at the refreshing breeze.'   23

Kūtadanta said: 'I feel, Lord, that you proclaim a great doctrine, but I cannot grasp it. Bear with me that I ask again: Tell me, Lord, if there is no ātman, how can there be immortality? The activity of the mind passes, and our thoughts are gone when we have done thinking.' 24

Buddha replied: 'Our thinking is gone, but our thoughts continue. Reasoning ceases, but knowledge remains.'   25

Kūtadanta said: 'How is that? Is not reasoning and knowledge the same?'   26

The Blessed One explained the distinction by an illustration: 'It is as when someone wants, during the night, to send a letter, and, after having the clerk called, has a lamp lit, and gets the letter written. Then, when that has been done, the lamp is extinguished. But though the writing has been finished and the light has been put out the letter is still there. Thus does reasoning cease and knowledge remain; and in the same way mental activity ceases, but experience, wisdom, and all the fruits of our acts endure.'   27

Kūtadanta continued: 'Tell me, Lord, where, if the sankhāras are dissolved, is the identity of my self. If my thoughts are propagated, and if my soul migrates, my thoughts cease to be *my* thoughts and my soul ceases to be *my* soul. Give me an illustration, but please tell me where is the identity of my self?'   28

The Blessed One said: 'Suppose someone were to light a lamp; would it burn the night through?'   29

'Yes, it might do so,' was the reply.   30

'Now, is it the same flame that burns in the first watch of the night as in the second?'   31

Kūtadanta hesitated. He thought 'Yes, it is the same flame,' but fearing the complications of a hidden meaning, and trying to be exact, he said: 'No, it is not.'   32

'Then,' continued the Blessed One, 'there are flames, one in the first watch and the other in the second watch?'   33

'No, sir,' said Kūtadanta. 'In one sense it is not the same flame, but in another sense it is the same flame. It burns the same kind of oil, it emits the same kind of light, and it serves the same purpose.'   34

'Very well,' said the Buddha, 'and would you call those flames the same that have burned yesterday and are burning now in the same lamp, filled with the same kind of oil, illuminating the same room?'   35

'They may have been extinguished during the day,' suggested
Kūtadanta. 36

The Blessed One said: 'Suppose the flame of the first watch had been
extinguished during the second watch, would you call it the same if
it burns again in the third watch?' 37

Kūtadanta replied: 'In one sense it is a different flame, in another it is
not.' 38

The Tathāgata asked again: 'Has the time that elapsed during the
extinction of the flame anything to do with its identity or
nonidentity?' 39

'No, sir,' said the Brahman, 'it has not. There is a difference and
an identity, whether many years elapsed or only one second, and
also whether the lamp has been extinguished in the meantime
or not.' 40

VAJRASATTVA, THE SUPREME BUDDHA, THE PRINCIPLE OF
PURITY AND PURIFICATION. 17TH CENTURY, TIBET.

'Well, then, we agree that the flame of today is in a certain sense the same as the flame of yesterday, and in another sense it is different at every moment. Moreover, the flames of the same kind, illuminating with equal power the same kind of rooms, are in a certain sense the same.'   41

'Yes, sir,' replied Kūtadanta.   42

The Blessed One continued: 'Now, suppose there is a man who feels like yourself, thinks like yourself, and acts like yourself, is he not the same man as you?'   43

'No, sir,' interrupted Kūtadanta.   44

The Buddha said: 'Do you deny that the same logic holds good for yourself that holds good for the things of the world?'   45

Kūtadanta thought and continued slowly: 'No, I do not. The same logic holds good universally; but there is a peculiarity about my self which renders it altogether different from everything else and also from other selves. There may be another man who feels exactly like me, thinks like me, and acts like me; suppose even he had the same name and the same kind of possessions, he would not be myself.'   46

'True, Kūtadanta,' answered Buddha, 'he would not be yourself. Now, tell me, is the person who goes to school one, and that same person when finished with schooling another? Is it one who commits a crime, another who is punished by having hands and feet cut off?'   47

'They are the same,' was the reply.   48

'Then sameness is constituted by continuity only?' asked the Tathāgata.   49

'Not only by continuity,' said Kūtadanta, 'but also and mainly by identity of character.'   50

'Very well,' concluded the Buddha, 'then you agree that persons can be the same, in the same sense as two flames of the same kind are called the same; and you must recognize that in this sense another man of the same character and product of the same karma is the same as you.'   51

'Well, I do,' said the Brahman.   52

The Buddha continued: 'And in this same sense alone are you the same today as yesterday. Your nature is not constituted by the matter of which your body consists, but by your sankhāras, the forms of the body, of sensations, of thoughts. Your person is the combination of the sankhāras. Wherever they are, you are. To whatever place they go, you go. Thus you will recognize in a certain sense an identity of your self, and in another sense a difference. But one who does not recognize the identity should deny all identity, and should say that the questioner is no longer the same person as the one who a minute after receives the answer. Now consider the continuation of your personality, which is preserved in your karma. Do you call it death and annihilation, or life and continued life?'   53

'I call it life and continued life,' replied Kūtadanta, 'for it is the continuation of my existence, but I do not care for that kind of continuation. All I care for is the continuation of self in the other sense, which makes of every man, whether identical with me or not, an altogether different person.'   54

'Very well,' said Buddha. 'This is what you desire and this is the clinging to self. This is your error. All compound things are transitory: they grow and they decay. All compound things are subject to pain: they will be separated from what they love and be joined to what they abhor. All compound things lack a self, an ātman, an ego.'   55

'How is that?' asked Kūtadanta.   56

'Where is your self?' asked the Buddha. And when Kūtadanta made no reply, he continued: 'Your self to which you cling is a constant change. Years ago you were a small baby; then, you were a boy; then a youth, and now, you are a man. Is there any identity of the baby and the man? There is an identity in a certain sense only. Indeed there is more identity between the flames of the first and the third watch, even though the lamp might have been extinguished during the second watch. Now which is your true self, that of yesterday,

that of today, or that of tomorrow, for the preservation of which
you clamor?'   57

Kūtadanta was bewildered. 'Lord of the world,' he said, 'I see my error,
but I am still confused.'   58

The Tathāgata continued: 'It is by a process of evolution that
sankhāras come to be. There is no sankhāra which has sprung
into being without a gradual becoming. Your sankhāras are the
product of your deeds in former existences. The combination of
your sankhāras is your self. Wheresoever they are impressed
there your self migrates. In your sankhāras you will continue to live
and you will reap in future existences the harvest sown now and in
the past.'   59

'Certainly Lord,' responded Kūtadanta, 'this is not a fair retribution. I
cannot recognize the justice that others after me will reap what I am
sowing now.'   60

The Blessed One waited a moment and then replied: 'Is all teaching in
vain? Do you not understand that those others are you yourself?
You yourself will reap what you sow, not others.   61

'Think of a man who is ill-bred and destitute, suffering from the
wretchedness of his condition. As a boy he was slothful and
indolent, and when he grew up he had not learned a craft to earn a
living. Would you say his misery is not the product of his own
action, because the adult is no longer the same person as was the
boy?   62

'Not in the heavens, not in the midst of the sea, not if you hide
yourself away in the clefts of the mountains, will you find a place
where you can escape the fruit of your evil actions.   63

'At the same time you are sure to receive the blessings of your good
actions.   64

'"The one who has long been traveling and who returns home in
safety, the welcome of kinsfolk, friends, and acquaintances awaits.
So, the fruits of good works bid one welcome when one passes over
from the present life into the hereafter.'   65

Kūtadanta said: 'I have faith in the glory and excellency of your doctrines. My eye cannot as yet endure the light; but I now understand that there is no self, and the truth dawns upon me. Sacrifices cannot save, and invocations are idle talk. But how shall I find the path to life everlasting? I know all the Vedas by heart and have not found the truth.'   66

The Buddha said: 'Learning is a good thing; but it has no benefit. True wisdom can be acquired by practice only. Practise the truth that others are the same as you. Walk in the noble path of righteousness and you will understand that while there is death in self, there is immortality in truth.'   67

Kūtadanta said: 'Let me take my refuge in the Blessed One, in the Dharma, and in the Sangha. Accept me as your disciple and let me partake of the bliss of immortality.'   68

THE FEMALE DEVATA USNISAVIJAYA, SHOWING 8 ARMS.
18TH CENTURY, TIBET.

XXXII
One Essence, One Law, One Aim
*

THE TATHĀGATA ADDRESSED the venerable Kassapa in order to
dispel the uncertainty and doubt of his mind, and he said: 1
'All things are made of one essence, yet things are different according
to the forms which they assume under different impressions. As
they form themselves so they act, and as they act so they are.   2
'It is, Kassapa, as if a potter made different vessels out of the same
clay. Some of these pots are to contain sugar, others rice, others
curds and milk; others still are vessels of impurity. There is no
diversity in the clay used; the diversity of the pots is only due to the
moulding hands of the potter who shapes them for the various uses
that circumstances may require.   3
'And as all things originate from one essence, so they are developing
according to one law and they are destined to one aim which is
Nirvāna.   4
'Nirvāna comes to you, Kassapa, when you understand thoroughly,
and when you live according to your understanding, that all things
are of one essence and that there is but one law. Hence, there is but
one Nirvāna as there is but one truth, not two or three.   5
'And the Tathāgata recreates the whole world like a cloud shedding its
waters without distinction. He has the same sentiments for the high
as for the low, for the wise as for the ignorant, for the noble-minded
as for the immoral.   7
'The great cloud full of rain comes up in this wide universe covering
all countries and oceans to pour down its rain everywhere, over all
grasses, shrubs, herbs, trees of various species, families of plants of
different names growing on the earth, on the hills, on the
mountains, or in the valleys.   8
'Then, Kassapa, the grasses, shrubs, herbs, and wild trees suck the
water emitted from that great cloud which is all of one essence and
has been abundantly poured down; and they will, according to
their nature, acquire a proportionate development, shooting up and

producing blossoms and their fruits in season.   9

'Rooted in one and the same soil, all those families of plants and germs are quickened by water of the same essence.   10

'The Tathāgata, however, Kassapa, knows the law whose essence is salvation, and whose end is the peace of Nirvāna. He is the same to all, and yet knowing the requirements of every single being, he does not reveal himself to all alike. He does not impart to them at once the fulness of omniscience, but pays attention to the disposition of various beings.'   11

XXXIII
The Sermon on Abuse

＊

THE BLESSED ONE OBSERVED the ways of society and noticed how much misery came from malignity and foolish offences done only to gratify vanity and self-seeking pride.   1

And the Buddha said: 'If someone foolishly does me wrong, I will return to that person the protection of my ungrudging love; the more evil comes from such a person, the more good shall go from me; the fragrance of goodness always comes to me, and the harmful air of evil goes to that person.'   2

A foolish man learning that the Buddha observed the principle of great love which commends the return of good for evil, came and abused him. The Buddha was silent, pitying his folly.   3

When the man had finished his abuse, the Buddha asked him, saying: 'If a man declined to accept a present made to him, to whom would it belong?' And he answered: 'In that case it would belong to the man who offered it.'   4

The Buddha said, 'You have railed at me, but I decline to accept your abuse, and request you to keep it yourself. Will it not be a source of misery to you? As the echo belongs to the sound, and the shadow to the substance, so misery will overtake the evildoer without fail.' 5

The abuser made no reply, and Buddha continued: 6

'An evil person who reproaches a virtuous one is like one who looks up and spits at heaven; the spittle soils not the heaven, but comes back and defiles the person.   7

'The slanderer is like one who flings dust at another when the wind is contrary; the dust does but return on the one who threw it. The virtuous cannot be hurt and the misery that the other would inflict comes back on the slanderer.'   8

The abuser went away ashamed, but he came again and took refuge in the Buddha, the Dharma, and the Sangha.   9

XXXIV
The Buddha Replies to the Deva
✳

ON A CERTAIN DAY WHEN the Blessed One was at Jetavana, the garden of Anāthapindika, a celestial deva came to him in the shape of a Brahman whose countenance was bright and whose garments were white like snow. The deva asked questions which the Blessed One answered.   1

The deva said: 'What is the sharpest sword? What is the deadliest poison? What is the fiercest fire? What is the darkest night?'   2

The Blessed One replied: 'A word spoken in anger is the sharpest sword; covetousness is the deadliest poison; passion is the fiercest fire; ignorance is the darkest night.'   3

The deva said: 'Who gains the greatest benefit? Who loses most? Which armor is invulnerable? What is the best weapon?'   4

The Blessed One replied: 'The greatest gainer is one who gives to others, and the one who greedily receives without gratitude is the one who loses most. Patience is an invulnerable armor; wisdom is the best weapon.'   5

The deva said: 'Who is the most dangerous thief? What is the most precious treasure? Who is most successful in taking away by violence not only on earth, but also in heaven? What is the securest treasure-trove?'   6

The Blessed One replied: 'Evil thought is the most dangerous thief; virtue is the most precious treasure. The mind takes possession of everything not only on earth, but also in heaven, and immortality is its securest treasure-trove.'   7

The deva said: 'What is attractive? What is disgusting? What is the most horrible pain? What is the greatest enjoyment?'   8

The Blessed One replied: 'Good is attractive; evil is disgusting. A bad conscience is the most tormenting pain; deliverance is the height of bliss.'   9

The deva asked: 'What causes ruin in the world? What breaks off friendships? What is the most violent fever? Who is the best physician?'   10

The Blessed One replied: 'Ignorance causes the ruin of the world. Envy and selfishness break off friendships. Hatred is the most

SIMHANADA, A FORM OF AVALOKITESHVARA, SITTING ON THE
BACK OF A ROARING LION. 17TH CENTURY, TIBET.

violent fever, and the Buddha is the best physician.'   11

The deva then asked and said: 'Now I have only one doubt to be solved; please clear it away: What is it fire can neither burn, nor moisture corrode, nor wind crush down, but is able to reform the whole world?'   12

The Blessed One replied: 'Blessing! Neither fire, nor moisture, nor wind can destroy the blessing of a good deed, and blessings reform the whole world.'   13

The deva, having heard the words of the Blessed One, was full of exceeding joy. Clasping his hands, he bowed down before him in reverence, and disappeared suddenly from the presence of the Buddha.   14

XXXV
WORDS OF INSTRUCTION

❋

THE BHIKKHUS CAME TO THE Blessed One, and having saluted him with clasped hands they said: 1

'Master, we all wish to learn; our ears are ready to hear, you are our teacher, you are incomparable. Cut off our doubt, inform us of the blessed Dharma.   2

'We will ask the muni of great understanding, who has crossed the stream, gone to the other shore, is blessed and of a firm mind: How does a bhikkhu wander rightly in the world, after having gone out from his house and driven away desire?'   3

The Buddha said: 4

'Let the bhikkhu subdue his passion for human and celestial pleasures, then, having conquered existence, he will command the Dharma. Such a one will wander rightly in the world.   5

'He whose lusts have been destroyed, who is free from pride, who has overcome all the ways of passion, is subdued, perfectly happy, and of a firm mind. Such a one will wander rightly in the world.   6

'Faithful is one who is possessed of knowledge, seeing the way that leads to Nirvāna; one who is not a partisan; one who is pure and virtuous, and has removed the veil from the eyes. Such a one will wander rightly in the world.' 7

The bhikkhus said: 'Certainly, Bhagavat, it is so: whichever bhikkhu lives in this way, subdued and having overcome all bonds, such a one will wander rightly in the world.' 8

The Blessed One said: 9

'Whatever is to be done by those who aspire to attain the tranquillity of Nirvāna let them be able and upright, conscientious and gentle, and not proud. 10

'Let people's pleasure be the Dharma, let them delight in the Dharma, let them stand fast in the Dharma, let them know how to inquire into the Dharma, let them not raise any dispute that pollutes the Dharma, and let them spend time in pondering on the well-spoken truths of the Dharma. 11

'A treasure that is laid up in a deep pit profits nothing and may easily be lost. The real treasure that is laid up through charity and piety, temperance, self-control, or deeds of merit, is hid secure and cannot pass away. It is never gained by wronging others, and no thief can steal it. At death the fleeting wealth of the world must be left, but this treasure of virtuous acts is taken with one. Let the wise do good deeds; they are a treasure that can never be lost.' 12

And the bhikkhus praised the wisdom of the Tathāgata: 13

'You have passed beyond pain, you are holy, we consider you one that has destroyed the passions. You are glorious, thoughtful, and of great understanding. You who have put an end to pain, you have carried us across our doubt. 14

'Because you saw our longing and carried us across our doubt, adoration be to you, O muni, who have attained the highest good in the ways of wisdom. 15

'The doubt we had before, you have cleared away; surely you are perfectly enlightened, there is no obstacle for you. 16

'And all your troubles are scattered and cut off; you are calm, subdued, firm, truthful. 17

'Adoration be to you noble sage; in the world of human beings and gods there is none equal to you.   18

'You are the Buddha, you are the Master, you are the muni that conquers Mâra; after having cut off desire you have crossed over and carry this generation to the other shore.'   19

XXXVI
The Teacher Unknown
✽

THE BLESSED ONE said to Ānanda: 1

'There are various kinds of assemblies, Ānanda; assemblies of nobles, of Brahmans, of householders, of bhikkhus, and of other beings. When I used to enter an assembly, I always became, before I seated myself, in color like the color of my audience, and in voice like their voice. I spoke to them in their language and then with religious discourse, I instructed, stimulated, and gladdened them.   2

'My doctrine is like the ocean, having the same eight wonderful qualities.   3

'Both the ocean and my doctrine become gradually deeper. Both preserve their identity under all changes. Both cast out dead bodies upon the dry land. As the great rivers, when falling into the main, lose their names and are from then on reckoned as the great ocean, so all the castes, having renounced their lineage and entered the Sangha, become monks and are reckoned the sons of Sakyamuni. The ocean is the goal of all streams and of the rain from the clouds, yet is it never overflowing and never emptied: so the Dharma is embraced by many millions of people, yet it neither increases nor decreases. As the great ocean has only one taste, the taste of salt, so my doctrine has only one flavor, the flavor of emancipation. Both the ocean and the Dharma are full of gems and pearls and jewels, and both afford a dwelling place for mighty beings.   4

'These are the eight wonderful qualities in which my doctrine resembles the ocean.   5

'My doctrine is pure and it makes no discrimination between noble and ignoble, rich and poor.   6

'My doctrine is like water which cleanses all without distinction.   7

'My doctrine is like fire which consumes all things that exist between heaven and earth, great and small.   8

'My doctrine is like the heavens, for there is room in it, ample room for the reception of all, for men and women, boys and girls, the powerful and the lowly.   9

'But when I spoke, they did not know me and would say, "Who may this be who speaks so, a man or a god?" Then having instructed, stimulated, and gladdened them with religious discourse, I would vanish away. But they did not know me, even when I vanished away.'   10

✳

AVALOKITESHVARA, THE BODHISATTVA OF COMPASSION,
HOLDING A LOTUS BLOSSOM, A ROSARY AND A VASE OF
NECTAR. 17TH CENTURY, TIBET.

PARABLES AND STORIES

XXXVII
The Man Born Blind

◉

THERE WAS A MAN BORN BLIND, and he said: 'I do not believe in the world of light and appearance. There are no colors, bright or sombre. There is no sun, no moon, no stars. No one has witnessed these things.'   1

His friends remonstrated with him, but he clung to his opinion: 'What you say that you see,' he objected, 'are illusions. If colors existed I should be able to touch them. They have no substance and are not real. Everything real has weight, but I feel no weight where you see colors.'   2

In those days there was a physician who was called to see the blind man. He mixed four herbs to make a remedy, and when he applied them to the cataract of the blind man the grey film melted and his eyes acquired the faculty of sight.   3

The Tathāgata is the physician, the cataract is the illusion of 'I am,' and the four medicinal ingredients are the four noble truths.   4

XXXVIII
Vāsavadattā

◉

THERE WAS A COURTESAN in Mathurā named Vāsavadattā. She happened to see Upagutta, one of Buddha's disciples, a tall and beautiful youth, and fell desperately in love with him. Vāsavadattā sent an invitation to the young man, but he replied: 'The time has not yet arrived when Upagutta will visit Vāsavadattā.'   1

The courtesan was astonished at the reply, and she sent again for him, saying: 'Vāsavadattā desires love, not gold, from Upagutta.' But Upagutta made the same enigmatic reply and did not come.   2

A few months later Vāsavadattā had a love-intrigue with the chief of the artisans, and at that time a wealthy merchant came to Mathurā, who fell in love with Vāsavadattā. Seeing his wealth, and fearing the jealousy of her other lover, she contrived the death of the chief of the artisans, and concealed his body under a dunghill.   3

When the chief of the artisans had disappeared, his relatives and friends searched for him and found his body. Vāsavadattā was tried by a judge, and condemned to have her ears and nose, her hands and feet cut off, and flung into a graveyard.   4

Vāsavadattā had been a passionate girl, but kind to her servants, and one of her maids followed her, and out of love for her former mistress ministered to her in her agonies, and chased away the crows.   5

Now the time had arrived when Upagutta decided to visit Vāsavadattā.   6

When he came, the poor woman ordered her maid to collect and hide under a cloth her severed limbs; and he greeted her kindly, but she said with petulance: 'Once this body was fragrant like the lotus, and I offered you my love. In those days I was covered with pearls and fine muslin. Now I am mangled by the executioner and covered with filth and blood.'   7

'Sister,' said the young man, 'it is not for my pleasure that I approach you. It is to restore to you a nobler beauty than the charms which you have lost.   8

'I have seen with my own eyes the Tathāgata walking upon earth and teaching you his wonderful doctrine. But you would not have listened to the words of righteousness while surrounded with temptations, while under the spell of passion and yearning for worldly pleasures. You would not have listened to the teachings of the Tathāgata, for your heart was wayward, and you set your trust on the sham of your transient charms.   9

'The charms of a lovely form are treacherous, and quickly lead into temptations, which have proved too strong for you. But there is a beauty which will not fade, and if you will listen to the doctrine of our Lord, the Buddha, you will find that peace which you would have found in the restless world of defiled pleasures.'   10

Vāsavadattā became calm and a spiritual happiness soothed the tortures of her bodily pain; for where there is much suffering there is also great bliss.   11

Having taken refuge in the Buddha, the Dharma, and the Sangha, she died in pious submission to the punishment of her crime.   12

XXXIX
In the Realm of Yamarāja

THERE WAS A BRAHMAN, a religious man and fond in his affections but without deep wisdom. He had a son of great promise, who, when seven years old, was struck with a fatal disease and died. The unfortunate father was unable to control himself; he threw himself upon the corpse and lay there as one dead.   1

The relatives came and buried the dead child and when the father came to himself, he was so immoderate in his grief that he behaved like an insane person. He no longer gave way to tears but wandered about asking for the residence of Yamarāja, the king of death, humbly to beg of him that his child might be allowed to return to life.   2

Having arrived at a great Brahman temple the sad father went through certain religious rites and fell asleep. While wandering on in his dream he came to a deep mountain pass where he met a number of samanas who had acquired supreme wisdom. 'Kind sirs,' he said, 'can you not tell me where the residence of Yamarāja is?' And they asked him, 'Good friend, why do you want to know?' Whereupon he told them his sad story and explained his intentions. Pitying his self-delusion, the samanas said: 'No mortal

THANGKA PAINTING OF PADMASAMBHAVA. TIBET.

man can reach the place where Yama reigns, but some four hundred miles westward lies a great city in which many good spirits live; every eighth day of the month Yama visits the place, and you may see him there and ask for a boon.'   3

The Brahman rejoicing at the news, went to the city and found it as the samanas had told him. He was admitted to the dread presence of Yama, the King of Death, who, on hearing his request, said: 'Your son now lives in the eastern garden where he is amusing himself; go there and ask him to follow you.'   4

The happy father said: 'How does it happen that my son, without having performed one good work, is now living in paradise?' Yamarāja replied: 'He has obtained celestial happiness not for performing good deeds, but because he died in faith and in love to the Lord Buddha. The Buddha says: "The heart of love and faith spreads as it were a beneficent shade from the world of human beings to the world of gods." This glorious utterance is like the stamp of a king's seal upon a royal edict.'   5

The happy father hastened to the place and saw his beloved child playing with other children, all transfigured by the peace of the blissful existence of a heavenly life. He ran up to his boy and cried with tears running down his cheeks: 'My son, my son, do you not remember me, your father who watched over you with loving care and tended you in your sickness? Return home with me to the land of the living.' But the boy, while struggling to go back to his playmates, upbraided him for using such strange expressions as father and son. 'In my present state,' he said, 'I know no such words, for I am free from delusion.'   6

On this, the Brahman departed, and when he woke from his dream he thought of the Buddha, and resolved to go to him, lay bare his grief, and seek consolation.   7

Having arrived at the Jetavana, the Brahman told his story and how his boy had refused to recognize him and to go home with him.   8

And the World-honored One said: 'Truly you are deluded. When a person dies the body is dissolved into its elements, but the spirit is

DAINICHI NYORAI, THE 12TH/13TH CENTURY JAPANESE ZEN
MASTER OF THE RINZAI SCHOOL.

not entombed. It leads a higher mode of life in which all the relative terms of father, son, wife, mother, are at an end, just as a guest who leaves his lodging has done with it, as though it were a thing of the past. People concern themselves most about that which passes away; the end of life quickly comes as a burning torrent sweeping away the transient in a moment. They are like someone blind set to look after a burning lamp. The wise understanding the transiency of worldly relations, destroy the cause of grief, and escape from the seething whirlpool of sorrow. Religious wisdom lifts beings above the pleasures and pains of the world and gives them peace everlasting.'   9

The Brahman asked the permission of the Blessed One to enter the community of his bhikkhus, so as to acquire that heavenly wisdom which alone can give comfort to an afflicted heart.   10

XL
The Mustard Seed
◉

THERE WAS A RICH MAN who found his gold suddenly transformed into ashes; and he took to his bed and refused all food. A friend, hearing of his sickness, visited the rich man and learned the cause of his grief. And the friend said: 'You did not make good use of your wealth. When you hoarded it up it was no better than ashes. Now heed my advice. Spread mats in the bazaar; pile up these ashes, and pretend to trade with them.'   1

The rich man did as his friend had told him, and when his neighbors asked him, 'Why are you selling ashes?' he said: 'I offer my goods for sale.'   2

After some time a young girl, named Kisā Gotamī, an orphan and very poor, passed by, and seeing the rich man in the bazaar, said: 'My lord, why have you piled up gold and silver for sale.'   3

And the rich man said: 'Will you please hand me that gold and silver?' And Kisā Gotamī took up a handful of ashes, and lo! they changed back into gold.   4

Considering that Kisā Gotamī had the mental eye of spiritual knowledge and saw the real worth of things, the rich man gave her in marriage to his son, and he said: 'With many, gold is no better than ashes, but with Kisā Gotamī ashes become pure gold.'   5

And Kisā Gotamī had an only son, and he died. In her grief she carried the dead child to all her neighbors, asking them for medicine, and the people said: 'She has lost her senses. The boy is dead.'   6

At length Kisā Gotamī met a man who replied to her request: 'I cannot give you medicine for your child, but I know a physician who can.'   7

And the girl said: 'Tell me, sir; who is it?' And the man replied: 'Go to Sakyamuni, the Buddha.'   8

Kisā Gotamī went to the Buddha and cried: 'Lord and Master, give me the medicine that will cure my boy.'   9

The Buddha answered: 'I want a handful of mustard seed.' And when the girl in her joy promised to procure it, the Buddha added: 'The mustard seed must be taken from a house where no one has lost a child, husband, parent, or friend.'   10

Poor Kisā Gotamī now went from house to house, and the people pitied her and said: 'Here is mustard seed; take it!' But when she asked, 'Did a son or daughter, a father or mother, die in your family?' They answered her: 'Alas! the living are few, but the dead are many. Do not remind us of our deepest grief.' And there was no house in which some beloved one had not died.   11

Kisā Gotamī became weary and hopeless, and sat down at the wayside, watching the lights of the city, as they flickered up and were extinguished again. At last the darkness of the night reigned everywhere. And she considered the fate of beings, that their lives flicker up and are extinguished. And she thought to herself: 'How selfish am I in my grief! Death is common to all; yet in this valley of desolation there is a path that leads to immortality those who have surrendered all selfishness.'   12

Putting away the selfishness of her affection for her child, Kisā Gotamī had the dead body buried in the forest. Returning to the Buddha, she took refuge in him and found comfort in the Dharma, which is a balm that will soothe all the pains of our troubled hearts.   13

The Buddha said: 14

'The life of mortals in this world is troubled and brief and combined with pain. For there is not any means by which those that have been born can avoid dying; after reaching old age there is death; of such a nature are living beings.   15

'As ripe fruits are early in danger of falling, so mortals when born are always in danger of death.   16

'As all earthen vessels made by the potter end in being broken, so is the life of mortals.   17

'Both young and adult, both those who are fools and those who are wise, all fall into the power of death; all are subject to death.   18

'Of those who, overcome by death, depart from life, a father cannot save his son, nor kinsmen their relations.   19

'Mark! while relatives are looking on and lamenting deeply, one by one mortals are carried off, like an ox that is led to the slaughter.   20

'So the world is afflicted with death and decay, therefore the wise do not grieve, knowing the terms of the world.   21

'In whatever manner people think a thing will come to pass, it is often different when it happens, and great is the disappointment; see, such are the terms of the world.   22

'Not from weeping nor from grieving will anyone obtain peace of mind; on the contrary, one's pain will be the greater and one's body will suffer. One will make oneself sick and pale, yet the dead are not saved by one's lamentation.   23

'People pass away, and their fate after death will be according to their deeds.   24

'If a man live a hundred years, or even more, he will at last be separated from the company of his relatives, and leave the life of this world.   25

'Those who seek peace should draw out the arrow of lamentation,
and complaint, and grief.   26
'Those who have drawn out the arrow and have become composed
will obtain peace of mind; those who have overcome all sorrow will
become free from sorrow, and be blessed.'   27

THANGKA PAINTING SHOWING TSONGKHAPA, FOUNDER OF THE
GELUGPA SCHOOL OF TIBETAN BUDDHISM. TIBET.

THE LAST DAYS

XLI
The Buddha's Farewell Address

❊

THE BLESSED ONE went to Beluva, near Vesālī. There he addressed the monks, and said: 'Take up your abode for the rainy season round about Vesālī, each one according to the place where his friends and near companions may live. I shall enter upon the rainy season here at Beluva.' 1

When the Blessed One had entered upon the rainy season, there fell upon him a dire sickness, and sharp pains came upon him. But the Blessed One, mindful and self-possessed, bore his ailments without complaint. 2

Then this thought occurred to the Blessed One, 'It would not be right for me to pass away from life without addressing the disciples, without taking leave of the order. Let me now, by a strong effort of the will, subdue this sickness, and keep my hold on life till the allotted time has come.' 3

And the Blessed One, by a strong effort of the will subdued the sickness, and the sickness abated. 4

Thus the Blessed One began to recover; and when he had quite got rid of the sickness, he went and sat down on a seat spread out in the open air. And the venerable Ānanda, accompanied by many other disciples, approached where the Blessed One was, greeted him, and taking a seat respectfully on one side, said: 'I have observed, Lord, how the Blessed One was in health, and I have observed how the Blessed One had to suffer. And though at the sight of the sickness of the Blessed One my body became weak as a creeper, and the horizon became dim to me, and my faculties were no longer clear, yet notwithstanding I took some little comfort from the thought that the Blessed One would not pass away from existence until at least he had left instructions concerning the order.'   5

And the Blessed One said: 6

'What, then, Ānanda, does the order expect of me? I have preached
the truth without making any distinction between exoteric and
esoteric doctrine; for in respect of the truth, Ānanda, the Tathāgata
has no such thing as the closed fist of a teacher, who keeps some
things back.   7

'Surely, Ānanda, should there be anyone who harbors the thought, "It
is I who will lead the order," or, "The order is dependent upon me,"
he should lay down instructions in matters concerning the order.
Now the Tathāgata, Ānanda, does not think that it is he who should
lead the sangha, or that the order is dependent upon him.   8

'Why, then, should the Tathāgata leave instructions in any matter
concerning the order?   9

'I am now grown old, Ānanda, and full of years; my journey is
drawing to its close, I have reached the sum of my days, I am
turning eighty years of age.   10

'Just as a worn out cart cannot be made to move along without much
difficulty, so the body of the Tathāgata can only be kept going with
much additional care.   11

'It is only, Ānanda, when the Tathāgata, ceasing to attend to any
outward thing, becomes plunged in that devout meditation of heart
which is concerned with no bodily object, it is only then that the
body of the Tathāgata is at ease.   12

'Therefore, Ānanda, be lamps unto yourselves. Rely on yourselves, and
do not rely on external help.   13

'Hold fast to the truth as a lamp. Seek salvation alone in the truth. Do
not look for assistance to anyone besides yourselves.   14

'And how, Ānanda, can a monk be a lamp unto himself, rely on
himself only and not on any external help, holding fast to the truth
as his lamp and seeking salvation in the truth alone, looking not for
assistance to anyone besides himself?   15

' Ānanda, let a monk, as he dwells in the body, so regard the body that
he, being strenuous, thoughtful, and mindful, may, whilst in the

world, overcome the grief which arises from the body's cravings. 16

'While subject to sensations let him continue so to regard the sensations that he, being strenuous, thoughtful, and mindful, may, whilst in the world, overcome the grief which arises from the sensations. 17

'And so, also, when he thinks or reasons, or feels, let him so regard his thoughts that being strenuous, thoughtful, and mindful he may, whilst in the world, overcome the grief which arises from the craving due to ideas, or to reasoning, or to feeling. 18

'Those who, either now or after I am dead, shall be lamps unto themselves, relying upon themselves only and not relying upon any external help, but holding fast to the truth as their lamp, and seeking their salvation in the truth alone, and shall not look for assistance to anyone besides themselves, it is they, Ānanda, among my bhikkhus, who shall reach the very topmost height! But they must be anxious to learn.' 19

XLII
Chunda, the Smith

❀

AND THE BLESSED ONe went to Pāvā. 1

When Chunda, the worker in metals, heard that the Blessed One had come to Pāvā and was staying in his mango grove, he came to the Buddha and respectfully invited him and his disciples to take their meal at his house. And Chunda prepared rice cakes and a dish of dried boar's meat. 2

When the Blessed One had eaten the food prepared by Chunda, there fell upon him a dire sickness, and sharp pain came upon him. But the Blessed One, mindful and self-possessed, bore it without complaint. 3

The Blessed One said to Ānanda: 'Come, Ānanda, let us go on to Kusinārā.' 4

On his way the Blessed One grew tired, and he went aside from the road to rest at the foot of a tree, and said: 'Fold the robe please Ānanda, and spread it out for me. I am weary and must rest awhile!'   5

And Ānanda spread out the robe folded fourfold.   6

The Blessed One seated himself and said: 'Fetch me some water, Ānanda. I am thirsty and would like to drink.'   7

The venerable Ānanda said to the Blessed One: 'But just now, Lord, five hundred carts have gone across the brook and have stirred the water; a river is not far off. Its water is clear and pleasant, cool and transparent, and it is easy to get down to it. There the Blessed One may both drink water and cool his limbs.'   8

A second time the Blessed One said: 'Fetch me some water please Ānanda, I am thirsty and would like to drink.'   9

And a second time Ānanda said: 'Let us go to the river.'   10

Then the third time the Blessed One addressed the venerable Ānanda and said: 'Fetch me some water please, Ānanda, I am thirsty and would like to drink.'   11

'So be it Lord!' said Ānanda and, taking a bowl, he went down to the stream. And the stream, which had been muddy, now flowed clear and bright and free from all turbidity. And he thought: 'How wonderful, how marvelous is the great might and power of the Tathāgata!'   12

Ānanda brought the water to the Lord and the Blessed One drank. 13

Now, at that time a man of low caste, named Pukkusa, a young Malla, a disciple of Alāra Kālāma, was passing along the high road from Kusinārā to Pāvā.   14

And Pukkusa saw the Blessed One seated at the foot of a tree. He went up to the Blessed One, saluted him and took his seat respectfully on one side. Then the Blessed One instructed, edified, and gladdened Pukkusa, the young Malla, with discourse.   15

Aroused and gladdened by the words of the Blessed One, Pukkusa addressed a certain man who happened to pass by, and said: 'Please fetch me two robes of cloth of gold, burnished and ready for wear.'   16

As you wish that man said to Pukkusa and he brought two robes of
cloth of gold, burnished and ready for wear.   17
Pukkusa presented the two robes to the Blessed One, saying: 'Lord,
these two robes are ready for wear. May the Blessed One show me
favor and accept them!'   18
The Blessed One said: 'Pukkusa, robe me in one, and Ānanda in the
other.'   19
And the Tathāgata's body appeared shining like a flame, and he was
beautiful above all expression.   20
The venerable Ānanda said to the Blessed One: 'How wonderful a
thing it is, Lord, and how marvellous, that the color of the skin of
the Blessed One should be so clear, so exceedingly bright! When I
placed this robe of burnished cloth of gold on the body of the
Blessed One, it seemed as if it had lost its splendor!'   21
The Blessed One said: 'There are two occasions on which a Tathāgata's
appearance becomes clear and exceeding bright. In the night,
Ānanda, in which a Tathāgata attains to the supreme and perfect
insight, and in the night in which he passes finally away in that
utter passing away which leaves nothing whatever of his earthly
existence to remain.'   22
And the Blessed One then said: 'Now it may happen, Ānanda, that
someone should stir up remorse in Chunda, the smith, by saying: "It
is evil to you Chunda, and loss to you that the Tathāgata died, having
eaten his last meal from your provision." Any such remorse, Ānanda,
in Chunda, the smith, should be checked by saying: "It is good to you
Chunda, and gain to you that the Tathāgata died, having eaten his last
meal from your provision. From the very mouth of the Blessed One,
Chunda, have I heard, from his own mouth have I received this
saying, 'These two offerings of food are of equal fruit and of much
greater profit than any other: the offerings of food which a Tathāgata
accepts when he has attained perfect enlightenment and when he
passes away by the utter passing away in which nothing whatever of
his earthly existence remains behind–these two offerings of food are
of equal fruit and of equal profit, and of much greater fruit and much

greater profit than any other. There has been laid up by Chunda, the smith, a karma resulting in length of life, resulting in good birth, resulting in good fortune, resulting in good fame, resulting in the inheritance of heaven and of great power.' In this way, Ānanda, should be checked any remorse in Chunda.'   23

Then the Blessed One, perceiving that death was near, uttered these words: 'One who gives away shall have real gain. One who subdues oneself shall be free and shall cease to be a slave of passions. The righteous cast off evil; and by rooting out lust, bitterness, and illusion, reach Nirvāna.'   24

GILT-BRONZE FIGURE OF AN ELEPHANT WITH ENAMEL TRAPPINGS AND CORAL AND TURQUOISE CABOCHONS, TOGETHER WITH SADDLE CLOTH DECORATED WITH BUDDHIST EMBLEMS. C.1780, CHIEN LUNG PERIOD.

XLIII
Metteyya

*

THE BLESSED ONE PROCEEDED with a great company of disciples to the sāla grove of the Mallas, the Upavattana of Kusinārā on the further side of the river Hiraññavatī, and when he had arrived he addressed the venerable Ānanda, and said: 'Make ready for me, Ānanda, the couch with its head to the north, between the twin sāla trees. I am weary and wish to lie down.'   1

'As you say, Lord!' said the venerable Ānanda. The Blessed One laid himself down, and he was mindful and self-possessed.   2

Now, at that time the twin sāla trees were full of bloom with flowers out of season; and heavenly songs wafted from the skies, out of reverence for the successor of the Buddhas of old. And Ānanda was filled with wonder that the Blessed One was thus honored. But the Blessed One said: 'Not by such events, Ānanda, is the Tathāgata rightly honored, held sacred, or revered. But the brother or the sister, the devout man or the devout woman, who continually fulfils all the greater and the lesser duties, walking according to the precepts, it is they who rightly honor, hold sacred, and revere the Tathāgata with the worthiest homage. Therefore, Ānanda, be constant in the fulfilment of the greater and of the lesser duties, and walk according to the precepts; in that way, Ānanda, you will honor the Master.'   3

Then the venerable Ānanda went into the vihāra, and stood leaning against the doorpost, weeping at the thought: 'Alas! I remain a learner, one who has yet to work out his own perfection. And the Master is about to pass away from me – he who is so kind!'   4

Now, the Blessed One called his disciples, and said: 'Where is Ānanda?'   5

And one of them went and called Ānanda. Ānanda came and said to the Blessed One: 'Deep darkness reigned for want of wisdom; the world of sentient creatures was groping for want of light; then the Tathāgata lit the lamp of wisdom, and now it will be extinguished again, before he has brought it out.'   6

The Blessed One said: 7

'Enough, Ānanda! Do not be troubled; do not weep! Have I not already, on former occasions, told you that it is in the very nature of all things most near and dear to us that we must separate from them and leave them?   8

'The foolish conceive the idea of "self," the wise see there is no ground on which to build the idea of "self," thus they have a right conception of the world and well conclude that all compounds amassed by sorrow will be dissolved again, but the truth will remain.   9

'Why should I preserve this body of flesh, when the body of the excellent law will endure? I am resolved; having accomplished my purpose and attended to the work set me, I look for rest!   10

'For a long time, Ānanda, you have been every near to me by thoughts and acts of such love as never varies and is beyond all measure. You have done well, Ānanda! Be earnest in effort and you too shall soon be free from the great evils, from sensuality, from selfishness, from delusion, and from ignorance!'   11

And Ānanda, suppressing his tears, said to the Blessed One: 'Who shall teach us when you are gone?'   12

The Blessed One replied: 'I am not the first Buddha who came upon earth, nor shall I be the last. In due time another Buddha will arise in the world, a Holy One, a supremely enlightened One, endowed with wisdom in conduct, auspicious, knowing the universe, an incomparable leader of men, a master of angels and mortals. He will reveal to you the same eternal truths which I have taught you. He will preach his religion, glorious in its origin, glorious at the climax, and glorious at the goal, in the spirit and in the letter. He will proclaim a religious life, wholly perfect and pure; such as I now proclaim.'   13

Ānanda said: 'How shall we know him?'   14

The Blessed One said: 'He will be known as Metteyya, which means "he whose name is kindness."'   15

✳

GLOSSARY OF TERMS

IN THIS BOOK all unnecessary terms have been avoided. Whenever a good English equivalent could be found, the foreign expression has been dropped. Nevertheless, the use not only of many foreign sounding names, but also of some of the original terms, was unavoidable. Now we have to state that the Eastern people, at least those of Hindu culture during the golden age of Buddhism in India, adopted the habit of translating not only terms but also names. A German whose name is Schmied is not called Smith in English, but Buddhists, when translating from Pāli into Sanskrit, change Siddhattha into Siddhārtha. The reason of this strange custom lies in the fact that Buddhists originally employed the popular speech and did not adopt the use of Sanskrit until about five hundred years after Buddha. Since the most important names and terms, such as Nirvāna, Karma and Dharma, have become familiar to us in their Sanskrit form, while their Pāli equivalents, Nibbāna, Kamma and Dhamma, are little used, *it appeared advisable to prefer for some terms the Sanskrit forms*, but there are instances in which the Pāli, for some reason or other, has been preferred by English authors [e.g. Krishā Gautamī is always called Kisāgotamī], we present here in the Glossary both the Sanskrit and the Pāli forms.

Names which have been Anglicised, such as 'Brahmā, Brahman, Benares, Jain, and karma,' have been preserved in their accepted form. If we adopt the rule of transferring Sanskrit and Pāli words in their stem-form, as we do in most cases (e.g. Nirvāna, ātman), we ought to call Brahma 'Brahman,' and karma 'karman.' But *usus est tyrannus.* In a popular book it is not wise to swim against the stream.

Following the common English usage of saying 'Christ,' not 'the Christ,' we say in the title 'Buddha,' not 'the Buddha.'

Agni, *p.* and *skt.*, a god of the Brahmans, the god of fire.

Ambapā'li, the courtesan, called 'Lady Amra' in Fo-Sho-Hing-Tsan-King. It is difficult for us to form a proper conception of the social position of courtesans at Buddha's time in India. This much is sure, that they were not common prostitutes, but ladies of wealth, possessing great influence. Their education was similar to the hetairae in Greece, where Aspasia played so prominent a part. Their rank must sometimes have been like that of Madame Pompadour in France at the court of Louis XIV. They rose to prominence, not by birth, but by beauty, education, refinement, and other purely personal accomplishments, and many of them were installed by royal favor. The first paragraphs of Khandhaka VIII of the Mahāvagga [*S.B.*, Vol. XVII, pp. 171-172] gives a fair idea of the important rôle of courtesans in those days. They were not necessarily venal daughters of lust, but, often women of distinction and repute, worldly, but not disrespectable.

A'rahat, *p.*, Ar'hant, *skt.*, noble or holy being.

Arati, dislike, hatred. The opposite of *rati*. The name of one of Māra's daughters.

Ā'tman, *skt.*, Atta, *p.*, breath as the principle of life, the soul, self, the ego. To some of the old Brahman schools the ātman constitutes a metaphysical being in us which is the thinker of our thoughts, the perceiver of our sensations, and the doer of our doings. Buddha denies the existence of an ātman in this sense.

Benares, the well known city in India; Anglicised form of Vārānasī, *skt.*, and Bārānasī, *p.*

Bha'gavat, *p.*, Bha'gavant, *skt.*, the man of merit, worshipful, the Blessed One. A title of honor given to Buddha.

Bhi'kkhu, *p.*, bhi'kshu, *skt.*, mendicant, monk.

Bhi'kkhunī, *p.*, bhi'kshunī, *skt.*, nun.

Bodhisa'tta, *p.*, Bodhisa'ttva, *skt.*, one whose essence (*sattva*) is becoming enlightenment (*bodhi*). The term denotes (1) one who is about to become a Buddha, but has not as yet attained Nirvāna; (2) a class of being who has only once more to be born again to enter into Nirvāna; (3) in later Buddhism any preacher or religious teacher.

Bodhi tree, the tree at Bodh Gaya, species *ficus religiosa*.

Bra'hmā, Anglicised form of *skt.* stem form *Brahman* (nom. s. *Brahmā*). The chief God of Brahmanism, the world-soul.

Bra'hman, the priestly caste of the Indians. Anglicised form of *Brahmana* (*p.* and *skt.*). Priests were selected from the Brahman caste, but Brahmans were not necessarily priests; they were farmers, merchants, and often high officials in the service of kings.

Buddha, *p.* and *skt.*, the Awakened One, the Enlightened One. Buddha is also called Sakyamuni (the Sakya sage), Sakyasimha (the Sakya Lion), Sugata (the Happy One), Satthar, nom. Satthâ, *p.*; Shāstar, *skt.*, (the Teacher), Jina (the Conqueror), Bhagavat (the Blessed One), Lokanātha (the Lord of the World), Sarvajña (the Omniscient One), Dharmarāja (the King of Truth), Tathāgata, etc.

De'va, *p.* and *skt.*, any celestial spirit, a god especially of intermediate rank, angel.

Dha'rma, *skt.*, Dha'mma, *p.*, originally the natural condition of things or beings, the law of their existence, truth, then religious truth, the law, the ethical code of righteousness, the whole body of religious doctrines as a system, religion.

Dharmarā'ja, *skt.*, Dhammarā'ja, *p.*, the king of truth.

Go'tama, *p.*, Gau'tama, *skt.*, Buddha's family name.

Hīnayāna, *skt.*, the small vehicle, viz., of salvation. A name invented by Northern Buddhists, in contradiction to Mahāyāna, to designate the spirit of Southern Buddhism. The term is not used among Southern Buddhists.

Iś'vara, *skt.*, Ī'ssara, *p.*, (lit. independent existence) Lord, Creator, personal God, a title given to Shiva and other great deities. In Buddhistic scriptures as well as in Brahman the *skt.* Is'vara (not the *p.* Issara) means always a transcendent or extramundane god, a personal god, a deity distinct from, and independent of nature, who is supposed to have created the world out of nothing.

Jainism, a sect, founded by Vardhamāna, older than Buddhism and still extant in India. It is in many respects similar to Buddhism. Buddha's main objections to the Jains was the habit of their ascetics of going naked. The Jains lay great stress upon ascetic exercises and self-mortification which the Buddhists declare to be injurious.

Ji'na, *p.* and *skt.*, the Conqueror, an honorary title of Buddha. The Jains use the term with preference as an appellative of Vardhamāna whom they revere as their Buddha.

Ka'rma, Anglicised form of *skt.* stem form *ka'rman* (nom. s. *karma*), the *p.* of which is *ka'mmam*. Action, work, the law of action, retribution, results of deeds previously done and the destiny resulting therefrom.

Kha'ndha, *p.*, Ska'ndha, *skt.*, elements; attributes of being, which are form, sensation, perception, discrimination, and consciousness.

Kile'sa, *p.*, Kle'´sa, *skt.*, defilement.

Mahāyā'na, the great vehicle, viz., of salvation. Name of the Northern conception of Buddhism, comparing religion to a great ship in which beings can cross the stream of Samsāra to reach the shore of Nirvāna.

Mu'ni, *skt.* and *p.*, a thinker, a sage; especially a religious thinker. Sakyamu'ni, the sage of the Sakyas, is Buddha.

Nā'ga, *p.* and *skt.*, literally serpent. The serpent being regarded as a superior being, the word denotes a special kind of spiritual beings; a sage, a man of spiritual insight; any superior personality.

Nidā'na, *p.* and *skt.*, cause. The twelve nidānas, forming the chain of causation which brings about the misery in the world. [See Oldenberg, *Buddha*, Engl. tr., pp 224-252]

Nirvā'na, *skt.*, Nibbā'na, *p.*, extinction, viz., the extinction of self; according to the Hīnayāna it is defined as 'extinction of illusion,' according to the Mayāyāna as 'attainment of truth.' Nirvāna means, according to the latter, enlightenment, the state of mind in which upādāna, kilesa, and tanhā are extinct, the happy condition of enlightenment, peace of mind, bliss, the glory of righteousness in this life and beyond, the eternal rest of Buddha after death.

Ragā, pleasure, desire or lust; a synonym of *rati*. The name of one of Māra's daughters.

Rati, love, liking; a synonym of *ragā*. The name of one of Māra's daughters.

Sa'kya, *p.*, Sā'kya, *skt.*, the name of a royal race in the northern frontiers of Magadha.

Sakyamu'ni, *p.*, Śākyamu'ni, *skt.*, the Sākya sage; a cognomen of Buddha.

Sa'mana, *p.*, Srā'mana, *skt.*, an ascetic; one who lives under the vow.

Sammappadhā'na, *p.*, Samyakpradhā'na, *skt.*, right effort, exertion. There are four great efforts: (1) Mastery over the passions so as to prevent bad qualities from rising; (2) suppression of defiled thoughts to put away bad qualities which have arisen; (3) meditation on the seven kinds of wisdom in order to produce goodness not previously existing, and (4) fixed attention or the exertion of preventing the mind from wandering, so as to increase the goodness which exists. [See the Mahāpadhāna-Sutta in the *Digha-Nikāya*.]

Samsā'ra, *p.* and *skt.*, the ocean of birth and death, transiency, worldliness, the restlessness of a worldly life, the agitation of selfishness.

Sa'ngha, *p.* and *skt.*, the brotherhood of Buddha's disciples. The sangha forms the third constituent of the three jewels in which refuge is taken.

Sankhā'ra, *p.*, Samskā'ra, *skt.*, conformation, disposition. It is the formative element in the karma as it has taken shape in bodily existence.

Satipatthā'na, *p.*, Smrityupasthā'na, *skt.*, meditation; explained as 'fixing the attention.' The four objects of earnest meditation are: (1) the impurity of the body, (2) the evils arising from sensation, (3) ideas or the impermanence of existence, and (4) reason and character, or the permanency of the dharma.

Siddha'ttha, *p.*, Siddhā'rtha, *skt.*, Buddha's proper name. Etymology, 'He who has reached his goal.'

Tanhā, *p.*, Tr'ishnā, *skt.*, thirst; the word denotes generally all intense desire, clinging with passion. The name of one of Māra's daughters.

Tathā'gata, *p.* and *skt.*, generally explained as 'the Perfect One.' The highest attribute of Buddha.

Upādā'na, *p.* and *skt.*, desire, a grasping state of mind. One of the nidānas.

Va'ssa, *p.*, Va'rsha, *skt.*, rain, rainy season. During the rainy season of Northern India, which falls in the months from June to October, the samanas could not wander about, but had to stay in one place. It was the time in which the disciples gathered round their master, listening to his instructions. Thus it became the festive time of the year. In Ceylon, where these same months are the fairest season of the year, Buddhists come together and live in temporary huts, holding religious meetings in the open air.

Vihā'ra, *p.* and *skt.*, residence of Buddhist monks, a Buddhist convent or monastery; a Buddhist temple.

Ya'ma, *p.* and *skt.*, also called Yama-rā'ja, death, the king of death.

❁

REFERENCES

Abbreviations Used
in the Table of References

AN. – Añguttara Nikāya in Warren's Buddhism in Translations.

Bf. – Burnouf, Introduction à l'histoire du Bouddhisme Indien, Paris 1844.

BP. – Buddhaghosha's Parables. Translated by T. Rogers, London, 1870.

B St. – Buddhist Birth Stories or Játaka Tales. Translated by Rhys Davids.

CBS. – A Catena of Buddhist Scriptures from the Chinese by Samuel Beal. London, 1871.

Cb D. – [Chinese Dhammapada.] Texts from the Buddhist Canon, commonly known as Dhammapada. Translated by S. Beal, London and Boston, 1878.

Db. – The Dharma, or The Religion of Enlightenment by Paul Carus. 5th ed. Chicago, 1907.

DP. – The Dhammapada. Translated from Pāli by F. Max Müller, Vol. X, Part I, of the Sacred Books of the East. Oxford, 1881.

EA. – Explanatory Addition.

EH. – Handbook of Chinese Buddhism, by Ernest J. Eitel. London, 1888.

Fo. – The Fo-Sho-Hing-Tsan-King. A Life of Buddha by Asvaghosha, translated from Sanskrit into Chinese by Dharmarakhsha, A. D. 420, and from Chinese into English by Samuel Beal. Vol. XIX of the Sacred Books of the East. Oxford, 1883.

HM. – A Manual of Buddhism, by R. Spence Hardy.

MPN. – The Mahāparinibbāna Suttanta. The Book of the Great Decease. Vol. XI of the Sacred Books of the East. Oxford 1881.

MV. – The Mahāvagga. I-IV in Vol. XIII; V-X in Vol. XVII of the Sacred Books of the East. Oxford, 1881–1882.

Old G. – German Edition, Buddha, sein Leben, seine Lehre und seine Gemeinde, by H. Oldenberg. Second Edition. Berlin, 1890.

QKM. – The Questions of King Milinda, translated from Pāli by T.W. Rhys Davids, Vol. XXXV of the Sacred Books of the East. Oxford, 1890.

RB. – The Life of the Buddha from Thibetan Works, transl. by W.W. Rockhill. London, 1884.

rGya. – rGya Tchee Roll Pa, Histoire du Bouddha Sakya Mouni, by Foucaux. Paris, 1868.

RHB. – The Romantic History of Buddha from the Chinese Sanskrit, by S. Beal. London, 1875.

Rb DB. – Buddhism, by T.W. Rhys Davids, in the Series of Non-Christian Religious Systems. London, 1890.

S42S. – Sutra of Forty-two Sections. Kyoto, Japan.

SB. – Sacred Books of the East.

SN. – Sutta Nipāta, translated from the Pāli by V. Fausböll. Part II, Vol. X of the Sacred Books of the East. Oxford, 1881.

TPN. – Buddhistische Anthologie. Texte aus dem Pāli-Kanon. By Dr. Karl Eugen Neumann. Leyden, 1892.

US. – The Udāna by Major General D. M. Strong.

V. – Visuddhi-Magga in Warren's Buddhism in Translations.

W. – Buddhism in Translations by Henry Clarke Warren.

The original Pāli texts are published in the Journal of the Pāli Text Society, London, Henry Frowde.

The Table of References

ACKNOWLEDGEMENTS

THE PUBLISHERS would like to thank the following photographers and organisations for their kind permission to reproduce photographs in this book: The Bridgeman Art Library: pages 4 (National Museum of India, New Delhi); 37 & 45 (British Museum, London); 53 & 73 (Board of Trustees of the Victoria & Albert Museum, London); pages 77 & 113 (Oriental Museum, University); 81, 89 & 115 (Christie's, London); 125 (Partridge Fine Arts, London). Werner Forman Archive: pages 13, 29, 49 & 69; 17, 25, 33, 41, 57, 61, 86, 93, 97, 101, 105 & 109 (Philip Goldman Collection, London); 21 (Musée Guimet, Paris); 65 & 119 (Bad Wildungen Museum, Germany).